T0154271

LAKE SUPERIOR

Lake Superior

LORINE NIEDECKER'S

POEM AND JOURNAL

ALONG WITH OTHER

SOURCES, DOCUMENTS,

AND READINGS

WAVE BOOKS

SEATTLE AND

NEW YORK

Published by Wave Books www.wavepoetry.com

Copyright © 2013 by Wave Books All rights reserved

"Lake Superior" from *Lorine Niedecker: Collected Works*, copyright 2002.
Reproduced with permission of University of California Press. "Lake Superior
Country" from *Lorine Niedecker: Woman and Poet* by the National Poetry
Foundation of Orono (Jenny Penberthy, ed.), copyright 1996. Reproduced with
permission of National Poetry Foundation. "Niedecker and the Evolutional
Sublime" by Douglas Crase appears by permission of the author. "On a Monument
to the Pigeon" by Aldo Leopold reprinted with permission of The Wisconsin
Society for Ornithology, Inc. Lorine Niedecker notes, letters to Cid Corman,
and excerpts from *Back Roads to Far Towns* (Bashō/trans. Cid Corman
and Kamaike Susumu) reprinted with permission of Bob Arnold.

Wave Books titles are distributed to the trade by
Consortium Book Sales and Distribution
Phone: 800-283-3572 / SAN 631-760x

This title is available in limited edition hardcover
directly from the publisher

Library of Congress Cataloging-in-Publication Data
Niedecker, Lorine.
Lake Superior : Lorine Niedecker's poem and journal,
along with other sources, documents, and readings.—1st ed.
p. cm.
ISBN 978-1-933517-66-7
I. Title.
PS3527.I6L35 2013
811'.54—dc22 2012022705

We would like to thank Jenny Penberthy for all of her work, and
for *Lorine Niedecker: Woman and Poet*, which was an inspiration
for this book. We also thank Bob Arnold, and the staff of the
Hoard Historical Museum, for their support and assistance.

Designed and composed by Quemadura
Printed in the United States of America

9 8 7 6 5 4 3

LAKE SUPERIOR

Lake Superior

In every part of every living thing
is stuff that once was rock

In blood the minerals
of the rock

*

Iron the common element of earth
in rocks and freighters

Sault Sainte Marie—big boats
coal-black and iron-ore-red
topped with what white castlework

The waters working together
   internationally
Gulls playing both sides

*

Radisson:
"a laborinth of pleasure"
this world of the Lake

Long hair, long gun

Fingernails pulled out
by Mohawks

*

(The long
canoes)

"Birch bark
    and white Seder
        for the ribs"

*

Through all this granite land
the sign of the cross

Beauty: impurities in the rock

*

And at the blue ice superior spot
priest-robed Marquette grazed
azoic rock, hornblende granite
basalt the common dark
in all the Earth

And his bones of such is coral
raised up out of his grave
were sunned and birch bark-floated
to the straits

*

Joliet

Entered the Mississippi
Found there the paddlebill catfish
come down from The Age of Fishes

At Hudson Bay he conversed in latin
with an Englishman

To Labrador and back to vanish
His funeral gratis—he'd played
Quebec's Cathedral organ
so many winters

*

Ruby of corundum
lapis lazuli
from changing limestone
glow-apricot red-brown
carnelian sard

Greek named
Exodus-antique
kicked up in America's
Northwest
you have been in my mind
between my toes
agate

*

Wild pigeon

Did not man
    maimed by no
        stone-fall

mash the cobalt
    and carnelian
        of that bird

*

Schoolcraft left the Soo—canoes
US pennants, masts, sails
chanting canoemen, barge
soldiers—for Minnesota

Their South Shore journey
            as if Life's—
The Chocolate River
            The Laughing Fish
and The River of the Dead

Passed peaks of volcanic thrust
Hornblende in massed granite
Wave-cut Cambrian rock
painted by soluble mineral oxides
wave-washed and the rains
did their work and a green
running as from copper

Sea-roaring caverns—
Chippewas threw deermeat
to the savage maws
"*Voyageurs* crossed themselves
tossed a twist of tobacco in"

*

Inland then
beside the great granite
gneiss and the schists

to the redolent pondy lakes'
lilies, flag and Indian reed
"through which we successfully
                    passed"

                    *

The smooth black stone
I picked up in true source park
        the leaf beside it
once was stone

Why should we hurry
        home

                    *

I'm sorry to have missed
        Sand Lake
My dear one tells me
        we did not
We watched a gopher there

Lake Superior Country

The agate was first found on the shores of a river in Sicily and named by the Greeks. In the Bible (Exodus) this semi-precious stone was seen on the priest's breastplate.

A rock is made of minerals constantly on the move and changing from heat, cold and pressure.

The journey of the rock is never ended. In every tiny part of any living thing are materials that once were rock that turned to soil. These minerals are drawn out of the soil by plant roots and the plant used them to build leaves, stems, flowers and fruits. Plants are eaten by animals. In our blood is iron from plants that draw it out of the soil. Your teeth and bones were once coral. The water you drink has been in clouds over the mountains of Asia and in waterfalls of Africa. The air you breathe has swirled thru places of the earth that no one has ever seen. Every bit of you is a bit of the earth and has been on many strange and wonderful journeys over countless millions of years.

Lake Superior *Country*

The agate was first found on the shores of a river in Sici-
ly and named by the Greeks. In the Bible (Exodus) this semi-
precious stone was seen on the priest's breastplate.

A rock is made of minerals constantly on the move and chang-
ing from heat, cold and pressure.

The journey of the rock is never ended. In every tiny part
of any living thing are materials that once were rock that
turned to soil. These minerals are drawn out of the soil
by plant roots and the plant used them to build leaves, stems,
flowers and fruits. Plants are eaten by animals. In our
blood is iron from plants that draw it out of the soil. Your
teeth and bones were once coral. The water you drink has
been in clouds over the mountains of Asia and in waterfalls
of Africa. The air you breathe has swirled thru places of
the earth that no one has ever seen. Every bit of you is
a bit of the earth and has been on many strange and wonderful
joornies over countless millions of years.

So — here we go. Maybe as rocks and I pass each other I
could say how-do-you-do to an agate. What I didn't foresee
was that the highway doesn't always run right next the lake
(Superior ~~and before that~~, Michigan) and that you can travel
almost entirely around Superior (we didn't do the south shore
i.e. Copper Harbor) without finding more than a couple of ac-
cessible beaches. Where you can with some difficulty walk
over that terraine to the shore you suddenly find you're
on a high bluff and how are you going to get way down to the
water. And you're whizzing along the highway with a glimpse
of beach but there's traffic behind and you simply continue
to whiz. Or the shore when you do get down ~~to it~~ is sand,
not pebbles.

First stop - Green Bay. Statue here of gray granite: "The
Spirit of the Northwest", sculptured by Lorado Taft's pupil,
Bedore. It represents three figures who had most to do with
Green Bay - Nicolas Perrot, commandant of the region known
as La Baye as early as 1684; Father Claude Allouez who es-
tablished a mission here in 1671; and the third figure, a
member of the Outagami tribe.

We remember others who came there more than three centuries
ago in long canoes (the big French canoes were 35 feet long),

So—here we go. Maybe as rocks and I pass each other I could say how-do-you-do to an agate. What I didn't foresee was that the highway doesn't always run right next the lake (Superior or Michigan) and that you can travel almost entirely around Superior (we didn't do the south shore i.e. Copper Harbor) without finding more than a couple of accessible beaches. Where you can with some difficulty walk over that terrain to the shore you suddenly find you're on a high bluff and how are you going to get way down to the water. And you're whizzing along the highway with a glimpse of beach but there's traffic behind and you simply continue to whiz. Or the shore when you do get down is sand, not pebbles.

First stop—Green Bay. Statue here of gray granite: "The Spirit of the Northwest", sculptured by Lorado Taft's pupil, Bedore. It represents three figures who had most to do with Green Bay—Nicolas Perrot, commandant of the region known as La Baye as early as 1684; Father Claude Allouez who established a mission here in 1671; and the third figure, a member of the Outagami tribe.

We remember others who came there more than three centuries ago in long canoes (the big French canoes were 35 feet long), rowed or paddled, sometimes sailed, by Indians or French *voyageurs* singing as they rowed or as they rested during a *pause* which occurred, if possible every half mile but usually much less often than that. And for two centuries fur, principally beaver, was the accepted currency. Nicolet came in 1634, exploring the country for furs for Champlain who founded Quebec. A century earlier still (1535) Jacques Cartier had discovered the St. Lawrence River. The Indians at Green Bay gave a feast in Nicolet's honor—120 beavers were the main course. In May, 1670 Perrot and Saudry returned to Montreal with furs. Nine hundred natives in the flotilla. A plethora of furs, so great an amount that prices were lowered, however. An Indian could buy a gun from the English for two beaver skins; the French demanded more skins.

9

By 1700 Perrot gave up his diplomatic policy for a military one since the Fox wars had begun. But Green Bay developed. . . . De Langlade built a fur trading post about 1745. By 1815 de Langlade and sons and sons-in-law all were working for John Jacob Astor for the American Fur Company.

The average canoe carried more than 5 tons of furs and supplies and was manned by 8 *voyageurs*. The boats used in interior lakes and rivers carried 1 or 2 tons and were manned by 6.

More about furs—in 1773 Peter Pond entered the St. Peter's (Minnesota) River. He trapped the following winter and went to Prairie du Chien with furs. He counted there 130 canoes, some from Mackinac and some from as far away as New Orleans. His descriptions of the canoes themselves: "hundred wate appease all made of Birch Bark and white Seder for the Ribs". For the season ending spring 1775 Pond recorded a profit of $20,000. (II, Notes)

We didn't take time in Green Bay to stop for the Roi-Porlier-Tank cottage with its slim French windows and pottery that Tank's wife brought with her from Holland and the linen and glass. I don't know for a fact if the cottage is still here.

Now into Michigan following the lake. Escanaba, Indian name for Land of the Red Buck, city of the April smelt jamboree and wood industries. The city supplied 100,000 square feet of birds' eye maple for the S.S. Queen Mary.

Between Gladstone on Little Bay de Noc and Manistique we stopped at a gravel pit where I picked up a couple of light gray pieces of rock with sky-blue bands. Shale? A kind of slate? Here in this hot gravel pit a white daisy was not only hanging on but doing very well, one plant in the gravel roadway. The same common white daisy we were to see—with purple patches of wild sweet peas (something, at least, in the vetch family) all over the North even tho this year all the land was exceptionally parched from terrific heat and lack of rain. These flowers were the most beautiful beside sandy roads on the edge of birch and pine woods. From now on we saw mostly forests, endless evergreens.

Manistique, Indian name for vermillion (the colored earth the Indians used —or worm, actually?—to paint their faces). We stayed overnight here. Mfg. city and resort.

> AL: *The natives pronounce it MAN isty.*
> I: *So be it.*

The North is one vast, massive, glorious corruption of rock and language— granite is underlaid with limestone or sandstone, gneiss is made-over granite, shale, or sandstone and so forth and so on and Thompsonite (or Thomsonite) is often mistaken for agate and agate is shipped in from Mexico and Uruguay and can even be artificially dyed in the bargain. And look what's been done to language!—People of all nationalities and color have changed the language like weather and pressure have changed the rocks.

Out of Manistique it grew dark when it should have been getting light—we are early risers on trips, by 6:00 we're out on the road, sometimes 5:30— almost too dark to see the beautiful up-and-down-pathways in the park at Cut River Bridge. It began to rain hard, the first for these people in a month or so.

Still raining at St. Ignace in the Mackinac country—and fog. We saw NOTHING here because of this weather except faintly a sign pointing toward a wall of dark mist: Big Mac Bridge. Al tells me this bridge, three miles long, over the Straits of Mackinac, is the longest bridge in the world. As for rocks, Wisconsin's Doty had described, a hundred or more years ago, the rock of Mackinac Island off there in the fog as a composite of broken limestone "whiter than any I ever saw, organic remains found in it". Couldn't prove it by us, no see 'em. We had read that St. Ignace is mostly of French descent. The second oldest settlement in Michigan. Freight docks. Nicolet came earlier than Father Marquette but it was the latter who established a missionary chapel here in 1671.

In 1679 La Salle's boat Griffon, with sail put in at St. Ignace on its way to Green Bay for furs and on the return journey disappeared without a trace. (III, Notes) Marquette's grave is here, his second grave.

Michilimackinac, Chippewa name for big turtle, was how the whole upper Lakes region was designated in that early day. Whenever anyone said Mackinac, he said Mackinac of Michilimackinac. Kenneth Robert's novel, *Northwest Passage*, has the governor saying: "It's the bottleneck of the Great Lakes. There isn't a mosquito anywhere near . . . Every pelt that comes from the northwest and every package of goods that goes there, has to pass through Michilimackinac." At the end of the American Revolution, Mackinac was ceded to America by the terms of the Treaty of Paris, 1783, but the English refused to evacuate the post—didn't till the Jay Treaty, 1796. It seems that Dousman had a distillery here (Hercules Dousman of Villa Louis at Prairie du Chien or a relative?). Dr. Beaumont did some of his experimenting on gastric juices at Fort Mackinac. Before that colorful history was ended, Forts had been built successively in two or three different places in that area, each one known as Fort Mackinac.

In an exhibit in one of the Wayside Parks in Michigan we found that Petoskey is the state stone. To me, a new one. The big story, of course, in the upper Pen. is, or was, iron and copper and three-fourths of the iron ore in the US is found in the Lake Superior region.

How does Sault Sainte Marie—for instance *Sault* become Soo? Indian-French-English. Well, at any rate, here we are at the Soo. We took an excursion trip thru the locks, were raised way up—20 feet—because Lake Superior is that much higher than Lake Huron. The temperature that day was over 90 and a distracting up and down sojourn between decks was that of the people with their children with ice cream cups and candy bars (after the loud speaker had just asked everyone to keep his seat and not crowd to the rails, etc.). In Brady Park beside the locks you watch the big ore-carrying ships passing thru and listen to the whistles of the big boats, answered by the place on shore that keeps a watch on the happenings. Some of the long lake boats have taken on the red color of the iron ore, except for the gleaming white superstructure fore and aft. In the middle is that long, long barge-like body. The freighters bring the iron ore of Lake Superior and the smelting plants in the east together. It was announced on our excursion that 23,000 tons of iron ore was carried by one of the boats just back of us.

A museum in the park which somehow we didn't see—we were looking for it on East Portage near Schoolcraft House. Not easy here to find points of interest. Are the Sault Ste. Marie, Michigan, people conscious of their history? They are quite unaware as persons of tourists. Perhaps they're tired of these crowds. In Brady Park I noticed the modern-looking rest room building, at first glance something like a Spanish mission house. It had flowered paths before it. Out at the locks on the edge of the water are arrowed rest room signs—you can see them as you look at the big boats. I wonder what an old voyageur would have thought of them. The arrows of our day and the momentary, unsinging pause.

13

Of Sault Ste. Marie, Michigan, Henry Clay said: "the remotest settlement in the US if not in the moon". Oldest permanent settlement in Michigan and third oldest surviving community in the US. Was French till 1762 when the English took possession. The American army built Fort Brady in 1823 and with that English and French reign ended in the Soo.

Schoolcraft House was built by Henry Rowe Schoolcraft in the 1820's. They tell us its colonial characteristics have long been obliterated and the doors now are boarded up. Schoolcraft was Indian Agent of the Territory, a geologist and something of a poet, a politician and an explorer. He married the Europe-educated daughter of an Indian woman. He took a great interest in the Indians, resenting their being called savage, and ordered that no liquor be given them—he himself was a temperance man. In his later years he was commissioned by the government to write six volumes on the history and manners of the Indian tribes at $30,000 a volume. He had written several books that were to serve as the basis for Longfellow's "Song of Hiawatha". At the request of Governor Cass, Schoolcraft made at least two trips to that part of the Northwest we now call Minnesota. On one of these trips at least, he was accompanied by Cass and several notables like Pike, Beltrami, Thompson, each a specialist in his field and explored on this long journey the beginnings of the Mississippi River, the general topography as they went along, possibilities of mining and even negotiated treaties with the Indians. A geologist, a traveler into Minnesota, the land of all those lakes, a man who wrote and sketched what he learned and saw—ah, a long shot, but could we swerve off our course a bit and from the Soo to Lake Itasca go west from Grand Marais or Duluth instead of directly home? How about from Grand Marais west to Ely, all that wilderness in which a twenty-year old account told me you saw ospreys catching fish and eagles swooping down to take the fish from the ospreys. And Jasper Park lay near Ely and Soudan. (Jasper, an opaque quartz, red, yellow or brown or a kind of blend of these colors).

Schoolcraft might have gone this way on one of his trips, on his way to Rainy Lake or Red Lake. But I wanted Two Harbors, the agate capital of the Lake Superior region, and more of a look at North Shore.

I had a lovely whitefish supper at Sault Ste. Marie, Michigan, followed by a grasshopper—in a cool hotel.

We were now ready to start circling "the shining big sea-water". The largest and purest of the Great Lakes. Rock bluffs and the highway cut thru rock. Bring on your purities and your impurities for it's the mixture of minerals— lava flow—and rock that creates their colors.

We had to wait in Sault Ste. Marie, Canada, however, till 10:00 a.m. when the banks open. In changing our money into Canadian—$100—we made a profit of $9.75. Turned out we didn't spend anywhere near $100.

The Canadian Sault Ste. Marie is larger and cleaner-looking than the Michigan city, tho at the waterfront the washings were strung high from roof-top to roof-top. Up where the stores are we heard French spoken like a brook over pebbles, and British-English. My basket-pocketbook gave out from weight of notebooks and stones so I bought another—made in Hungary. Failing to bring along enough shirts for Al we bought a Calcutta fabric (not at all expensive) made in Hong Kong. The word for the entire trip is International. From agate on. The journeying, the mixing and changing.

At last we were ready to start toward Wawa, known to us already (circulars) as the town with the large statue of a Canadian goose with its wings half spread. Not far from the Soo we passed masses of rock thru which the road had been cut—whitish with splotches and flows of pink-red. I shouted "Oh" and could only think of marble. My manual tells me marble began as soft limestone and then heated by magma changed into many colors depending on the color of the sediment out of which it originally formed. Later I was told by someone who knows that what I'd seen must be granite. In some places as we went on, in certain light the rocks looked greenish.

For hundreds of thousands of years, geologists tell us, immense flows of lava —magma—covered the site of Lake Superior. Granite cooled more quickly than other kinds of rocks, giving it a finer grain.

Road signs are small in Canada.

> AL: *What did the sign say?*
> I: *What sign?*

I didn't miss the Agate Shop sign. Woman there knew rocks, whole store of all kinds of samples, labelled. Sold them cheaply too, i.e. agates mounted on adjustable rings cost $1.75. I bought one of these, not the most beautiful but a Lake Superior one, I was told. Also bought a blue stone, sodilite, un-mounted, an Ontario product, and a brilliant carnelian from Uruguay. There were corundum samples—also from Canada, the stone that is next to dia-monds in hardness. (Deep red rubies, which are corundum minerals, are valued more than diamonds.) (IV, Notes)

Picked up stones before Wawa, reddish and one green. Often on the trip the stones that had a shine turned out to be bottle caps.

Toward White River a sign: MOOSE CROSSING. If only we could see a moose —might be as big as a horse—without colliding with it as one can with deer back home. But no, the only animals we saw on the entire trip were dead porcupines on the road, and as at home, dead skunks.

Traffic not too heavy in Canada. Gasoline—5 quarts to a gallon and about 50c a gallon.

Up early at the White River motel, I heard the same birdsong, a wavy couple of notes, that I hear at home from across the river. Something the whippoor-will says, or nighthawk or what—I've never been nearer that sound than across a river, as I think I was even here in Canada.

Marathon on Heron Bay, next door to Terrace Bay, a pulp manufacturing plant, a pretty scene in early morning—dark streams out of the smoke-stacks, the only movement. A boat was tied at shore, as big as a fishing boat at Milwaukee, and a boom had been laid out to keep the sticks within a cer-tain area. At Lake Nipigon we saw Cameron Falls with a sluiceway for sticks to ride down into the lake to be picked up farther on by a boat. We probably should have driven all the way around Nipigon, a matter of about 70 miles.

Ouimet (we-met) Canyon—a tiny sign pointing in to a grave side road. I re-membered: Jasper! Away we gaily went. Soon a sign saying 6 miles and we began to have doubts about the road—so narrow I couldn't see how we could pass a car or turn around if we wanted to and I began to think I did. Al said the road wasn't as narrow as all that. On we went, the muscles in the back of my neck tensing with as they say: some unknown fear. A strain, it turned out, but mainly on the family tie—at first Al didn't want to go, I did, now I didn't and he did. It must have been much, much longer than 6 miles. Al says those little Canadian signs point and then after you get going there'll be a sign saying 70 miles! But beautiful if one could relax. Canada woods can be very quiet. Birch and purple and white flowers and ferns. It probably was a little more than 6 miles. When we got to a wider spot there we saw a school bus standing and young people. We were so done in we did not even get out and investigate, simply turned around and drove back out. This trip queered all side roads for us for the entire trip.

We mailed postcards from Nipigon which arrived back home almost a week later. By dog-team?

Endless miles of evergreen forests with tamarack near the road. Openings for small, perfect, picture-postcard lakes, evergreens solid to the water's edge. And these lakes are perfectly still, no boat, no person, no fish jumping. But the clearest, bluest water. No birds seen anywhere on the trip except gulls in plenty at the Soo and a few crows in Ontario.

At one place, almost hidden in the trees a sign: Post Office, and it pointed into the forest! *There* was one side trip we could afford to miss.

Apparently beside the highway every so often they have headquarters—fine looking buildings—for Mounties. We saw no mounties on horseback. We passed at one place a rather new building called First Aid Station.

No beer in Canada. Only Liquor Stores but they had no bars and tourists as a rule carry no ice. Soo, Canada, had hotels that didn't open till almost noon and then—we knew from experience—the men's and women's bars were separate. Women may not enter the men's barroom.

Port Arthur—stayed overnight here. TV from England—"The Common-wealth Festival of the Arts"—without commercials! Port Arthur still uses trolley buses.

Fort William—they've planted, the city, presumably, birch trees on the street terraces as maples or elms are planted in Milwaukee. Al, as we drove thru this city: "I wonder where the house is that was my Aunt Mary's (h)'ore-house". We looked toward the harbor here and did so at Ft. Wm. and knew that the ships were big and much went on there.

Looked like Taconite on the shoulder of the hard surface road out of Fort William—grayish with a slight reddish cast. (V, Notes)

At the International boundary we were asked "Are you naturalized citizens of the United States?" And "Did you buy anything?" We handed back the slip that had been filled out at the Michigan-Canada boundary. It seems you can buy $100 worth without paying customs fees.

Now we're at Pigeon River, so deeply associated in the mid-1600's with Radisson and his brother-in-law Groseilliers (Grosaya). As Walter Havighurst in our day says, "No Englishman would be expected to pronounce Groseilliers", therefore much of that region, river, falls and even now a state park carries the name the people gave it—Gooseberry. At any rate, scouting and fur-trading for Champlain, Radisson exclaimed, "We were Cesars, nobody to contradict us". On one occasion when they turned back to the St. Lawrence, they travelled at the head of 360 canoes laden with peltry. Radisson spoke of the Great Lakes world as "a laborinth of pleasure . . . the country so pleasant, so beautiful and fruitful it grieves me to see ye world could not discover such inticing countryes to live in. This I saw because the Europeans fight for a rock in the sea against each other." In the 1650's he described Sault de Ste. Marie and its fisheries, the Pictured Rocks and Chequamegon Bay where he and Groseilliers built the first known dwelling of white men on the lake. The winter of 1659–60 they spent up a little inland lake, probably Lac Court Oreilles in Sawyer Country, Wis., to which a trail led long after these men were dead and gone. Radisson had no fingernails— pulled off by the Mohawks when they bound him to a stake for slow killing. (These Frenchmen at Knife Lake—VI Notes)

A tiny restaurant at Cross River in Schroeder served butter in a dish always standing on the table from one person or family to another, also the jelly glass with spoon in it. We were hungry enough to use the butter but could not bring ourselves to touch the jelly. Coming out, we saw the Cross River Falls on the other side of the road.

At Grand Marais there is a tempting side road to Thompsonite Beach where I suppose one might with good luck and a lot of patience still be able to find a Thompsonite (Thomsonite) stone—a semiprecious gem, dark green with a pinkish spot—of course it wouldn't look like that in the raw. But no to side roads.

We spoke of starting west into Minnesota as soon as we could (my wish was being granted)—to Ely. There is mention in a 20-year old account of that wilderness of ospreys catching fish and eagles swooping down to take the fish from the ospreys. And Jasper Park lay near Ely and Sudan. But all the same I wanted Two Harbors, the agate capital of the Lake Superior Region. Even tho by now, of course, the capital may have shifted anyhow—agates were probably coming in from South America and Mexico. Could agates be commercially dyed?

And so it proved—altho after we found a public beach I was happy for a time. This was after the Gift Shop there which had some polished stones, i.e. Apache Tears, Labradorite, something black with lacey figures in it, amethyst and agate-ized wood. But the beach—the sign said LOOSE SAND into which the car got stuck. I ran to the shore while a young man helped Al get out. Later Al told me the man was a D. P. and that he carried a pick and hammer and had a pail of stones! Dear heaven, I could have been learning from him—undoubtedly a college student!

Oh well—now we were going right on thru Duluth, the city of the hilly streets, on west, in beside or near the St. Louis River, called in Schoolcraft's time, the Fond du Lac, the very stream he came in on, mentioning in his notes that here they found a man who had cows and it was a great treat in the wilderness to get this milk.

Minnesota, meaning "land of sky-tinted waters".

Iron, the most important geologic fact in Minnesota altho the limestone plays a big part in the state's story. A great arm, we're told, reached over here from the Atlantic and sediments formed sandstone, limestone and shale. To the glaciers Minnesota owes its fertile, pulverized limestone that has made wheat-raising lucrative. Reddish soil was pushed up from Illinois and pinkish from Labrador. From north of Lake Superior came gray-lavender drift which picked up rust from iron. In the northwest part of the state the retreating ice left a large body of water, larger than all the Great Lakes together, discovered by Agassiz in 1840—dried up in more recent geologic times. (VII, Notes)

Al has always headed the list of flowers peculiar to Minnesota with wild roses—"Not anywhere so big and healthy and rose-like as in northern Minnesota." Schoolcraft speaks of the numerous wild roses. All the books speak of them and blackberries, New Jersey Tea, bunchberries, pink and white lady slipper, Labrador Tea, thimbleberries, prairie phlox. . . .

But back to Schoolcraft and his party including Governor Cass, and Pike, Beltrami, Thompson, specialists in their fields, and Doty, a recorder of the 1820 trip. They left the Mackinac country with three canoes complete with masts, sails, a US pennant on each one, chanting canoe-men and accompanied by a 12-oar barge and 22 soldiers. At St. Mary's River at the Soo between the two separate villages "our flags flying, our little squadron being spread out in order and the Canadian boatmen singing one of their enlivening songs". Those on shore "fired a salute, and stood ready to greet us with their customary *Bosho*." Here's your language!—*bosho* for *bon jour*!

We have their comments, for this trip Doty's largely, reflecting the glorious but strenuous journey in and out of Lake Superior's southern shore. (XIII, Notes)

A lake in or near the St. Louis River turned out to be remarkable for its fine carnelians and agates—they named it Carnelian Lake. Over in the scrub oak prairies they spent a day and a half hunting buffalo —"The buffalo meat is rather inferior to that of the bear." On one of the gravely banks as they went on into the Minnesota River Valley (then called St. Peter's) Schoolcraft found a piece of agate-ised wood. It was noted that white sandstone overlaid with secondary limestone appears at St. Anthony's Falls—the first time since Lake Superior.

The discovery of the source of the Mississippi had to wait till Schoolcraft's 1832 trip. By this time the big canoes were a couple of inches shorter than the oldtime French type but no heavier for he speaks of portages where each man carried a canoe with its apparatus. He speaks his admiration for the working crew, how "they could set up a tent with its furniture in no time at all—he who would travel fast over an intricate interior route and be well served on the way, should not fail to prepare himself with a canoe allege and a crew of *voyageurs*. They will not only go when they are bid to go but they will go unmurmuringly. And after submitting to severe labor, both of the night and day, on land and water, they are not only ready for further efforts, but will make them, under the enlivening influence of a song."

At last the joyous discovery—Lake Le Biche (Elk Lake)—renamed by Schoolcraft, Itasca. He took the letters of this word from the latin *veritas ca-*

put, meaning true source. On July 13, 1832 he raised the American flag on an island in the lake now known as Schoolcraft Island. Now the whole area with a road 15 miles long forms a beautiful state park, a vast evergreen and birch woods. Nicolett came soon after, determining the latitude and longitude of the place. (IX, Notes)

I took a snapshot of the sweet little swampy place where the great river rises, a pond with water rushing into it from a culvert and over rocks. Nearby on a post: "Here 1475 feet above the ocean the mighty Mississippi begins to flow on its winding way 2552 miles to the Gulf of Mexico." A museum on the grounds contains exhibits of the formation of the Earth as it pertains to Itasca and of the kinds of wildlife found here. "Glaciers went over this area 4 times in the last million years", one of the exhibits said. The white-throat, we find, nests here, also the ruffled grouse and the scarlet tanager.

> I: *I don't see where the sun was all that time the glacier was going over.*
> AL: *It came down from the Polar cap. The sun was where it is now. When ice melts it moves forward or down.*

At one point in his accounts, Schoolcraft mentions Itasca as the primary source and names the secondary sources as Ossowa, The Long Water, source of a primary tributary of the Mississippi, Corbeau or Crow-Wing; and Shiba Lake and river, the source of Leech Lake.

The pebble has traveled. Long ago it might have been a drop of magma, molten rock that poured out from deep inside the earth. Perhaps when the magma cooled it formed part of a mountain that was later worn down and carried away by a rushing stream. Or the pebble may have been carried thousands of miles by a slowly moving glacier that finally melted and left it to be washed up for someone to pick up. It has traveled to many places and has been part of many things.

The sea went over and left me dry, parched for knowledge! The feeling of being a part of all this. How?—the body, the unconscious. Let us sing, as they say in church.

Meanwhile, knock about some more, touch the rough stones and some of the polished ones.

Jewelry? I seldom wear it.

Schoolcraft explored Cass Lake, Leech Lake (thru which the Miss. runs?) and several others. (XI, Notes) He was thinking of Governor Cass of Michigan Territory when he named the former Cassina. Later it was called simply Cass. I was sorry to miss his Carnelian Lake and Sandy Lake altho Al says we were at Sandy three years ago, he remembers watching a gopher there.

I suppose Schoolcraft must have seen Winnibigoshish, a large lake, 10 miles broad, which the Mississippi hits (runs thru it), near its source, as it runs north—can't make up its mind whether to turn south. We saw at Winnibigoshish the reservoir-dam that controls water in the Mississippi. I picked up a couple of small greenish stones and flat black.

Lake Bemidji—here the word is Paul Bunyan, a statue of him 18 feet tall and the blue ox. In the little park on the lake the trash barrels have painted on them the words: Paul Bunyan. All is big up in this country! Lumberjacks acknowledge Bunyan the ruler of the woods from the Winter of the Blue Snow to the Spring the Rain Came Up from China.

Leech Lake—after eating at Walker—named by the Indians for a huge leech that according to legend they once beheld swimming in the water. Leech is the third largest lake in Minnesota—40 miles across. Norway and white pine all thru here, now as when Schoolcraft saw it. Picked up greenish stones and brownish washed up along the edge of the water. I may have what the manuals call a rippled pattern in the brown stone. Presumably waves washed shores and rain showered down millions of years ago—causing a ripple pattern—just as today. Yet for all I know it could be not rock at all but a kind of shell or even a piece of present-day commercial detritus. Some dead white fish lay along the shore.

Bow-String Lake is not far away but we did not go there. Schoolcraft's mention of it in connection with negotiating an Indian treaty. Note also his def. of an Ind[ian]. (Notes X)

We saw Swan River again, Al's old home, nothing left on the spot where he spent his childhood and youth except the grove. Over near the depot is a root cellar, built more above ground, it seemed, than most, its upright door open. I thought it worthy of a snapshot. Maybe somebody would use it now as a tornado cellar. Never necessary I hope as a future bomb shelter.

Swan Lake is nearby. In 1851 Indians and whites came from all over the midwest to a treaty meeting at the mouth of the Minnesota, Traverse des Sioux. Chief Sleepy Eyes came from his beloved Swan Lake. (XI, Notes)

We started home. Brainard on the Mississippi (XII, Notes). Lake St. Croix— Schoolcraft sang the praises of this lake. The moon came out before they encamped. "If 'Loch Katrine' (Scotland) presents a more attractive outline of sylvan coast, it must be beautiful indeed. We went up it, turning point after point, with the pleasure that novelty imparts . . . Nothing could present a greater contrast to the noisy scene of horses and horsemen, war and bloodshed, which we were then unconscious was being enacted, so near to us." He referred to the capture of Black Hawk's band at the Bad Axe.

St. Croix Falls—Schoolcraft—"The river tears its way through a vast bed of greenstone, whose black and square masses stand on either side, and in the bed of the stream—common quartz, imperfectly crystallized is seen in the mass, and is the sole mineral apparent . . ."

The Snake River—yes it does wind. One last reminder of Schoolcraft, his story of an old man's. (XIII, Notes). Pine City—the Snake River runs thru the town. Along the river from its lake source in the St. Croix are basaltic lava flows. Copper prospectors used to live here.

A short distance above St. Anthony's Falls (now flooded over—at St. Paul and Minneapolis) the Rum River empties into the Corbeau or Crow-Wing. An early explorer thru here, Carver, found this river whose name contained the word *esprits*. French for spirits, good feelings, gods. Carver apparently did not understand the true meaning since he named the river Rum. The English and the French just did not get along!

Other entertaining stories of persons and places in old Minnesota. (XIV, Notes)

We stayed the last night at Little Falls, Minnesota, Lindbergh's old home town. Here Al bought some salami. Restaurant living was beginning to pall.

    I: *Good. It even shines a little.*
    AL: *That's from the horses' hooves—horsemeat maybe?*

The next day Home. The air grew hotter. The gravel along the highways lost its sparkle. We got so tired—Al from the strain of driving, that stream of cars. We thought at one time as a sign appeared that we were coming to the town of DO NOT PASS. At Tomah we entered the expressway and got the ride of our lives. Not so much traffic on this superhighway but fast-moving. We passed cars at 80 miles an hour and they passed us at close to 90.

When we reached Fort Al could hardly raise a glass to his mouth, his arm shook so much.

"Notes" are Niedecker's own. They are available in the University of Wisconsin Digital Collections.

Niedecker and the
Evolutional Sublime

DOUGLAS CRASE

Poetry is words. Yet when I think of the Whitman who found he incorporates gneiss, the Stein who says anybody is as their land and air is, the Stevens who locates mythology in stone out of our fields or from under our mountains, then I have to admit that the sublimest American poetry has always read to me as if it would rather restore, or even realize its desire for a wealth outside words, a wealth that is wild outside the human voice. That is what I always liked about it. It is what I liked at once about Lorine Niedecker's "Lake Superior," that spare ferropastoral of a poem in honor of the rock and mineral wealth

Iron the common element of earth

for which the human species is just another mode of transport. I also have to admit that what I like about our poetry may be exactly what makes it so alien to other readers. I remember vividly the disapproval of a reviewer who once noted in a British journal that the heroes of "Lake Superior" seem to be rocks, not men, but went on to judge "repellent" this same bias, this same extraspecies deference, that I read as honestly sublime.

28

The sublime is a term that does not come unembarrassed into American discourse. But sublime doesn't have to mean ultimate, and there is no inherent reason why a mention of the sublime has to be less practical, say, than a reference to the lyric. The sublime too ought to describe itself in traditions, and in the poetic practices implied by those traditions. In England the poetry of the egotistical sublime took shape, and probably impetus, from its tension with the social order. The poet, as Wordsworth was careful to add in the 1802 Preface to the *Lyrical Ballads*, was an individual who nonetheless spoke in a community: "the rock of defence for human nature," to use his exact words, who "binds together . . . the vast empire of human society." In America, Emerson left the binding—and the ego—out of the sublime. The poet, he wrote in the 1841 essay of that name, is one who apprises us not of personal wealth, but "of the commonwealth." Emerson too was careful with words, and I suppose it is almost diagnostic that he would reject words like empire and society, and, with Wordsworth's prior example in mind, identify the poet's material as a commonwealth instead. Because at its most reductive

Iron the common element of earth

the commonwealth is the land.

The line I have quoted twice is Niedecker's, of course, from "Lake Superior." The poem itself appeared complete in England in 1968, then remained for all practical purposes unavailable in the United States until its publication seventeen years later in *The Granite Pail* and *From This Condensery*, those two very different collections of Niedecker's work. Even today the poem may come as a surprise to readers who encounter it for the first time in the third *Norton Anthology of American Literature*, where its inclusion is both just and a little ironic. As another apprisal of the commonwealth, "Lake Superior" extends a tradition that seems peculiarly American, a tradition we honor only partway. For the truth is that when our poets start telling us about gneiss, or land and air, when they locate their story in stone or, as Niedecker does, in rock, I think we are likely to allow them the trope but not likely to believe they are saying what they in fact just said. They and their poems are made of land and air and rock. People who read poetry have always been alert enough to entertain the trope while avoiding the notion itself as sentimental, romantic or, worse, perniciously near to nationalism.

Get them away from poetry, however, and today's readers are also alert enough ecologically to know that their own identification with the environment isn't ipso facto proof of direct-mail mysticism or gang nationalism. In 1945, twenty-one years before she began work on "Lake Superior," Niedecker had written to Louis Zukofsky that she was reading Diderot. "This is what I could have used long ago," she reported, "alongside Engels and while I was wondering what Emerson was getting at. . . . Elements for awhile before we again become, if we ever do, another mass. Time is nuttin in the universe." It's a summary formulation, but it is hardly repellent. On the contrary, it reminds me agreeably of the presence in Wisconsin in those years of another commentator on the earthly commonwealth, one who sat down in his university office in Madison shortly before Christmas of 1941 to write an article, "Odyssey," that would appear the next summer in *Audubon* magazine, and again in 1949 as one of the now famous sections of *A Sand County Almanac*.

> An atom at large in the biota is too free to know freedom; an atom back in the sea has forgotten it. For every atom lost to the sea, the prairie pulls another out of the decaying rocks. The only certain truth is that its creatures must suck hard, live fast, and die often, lest its losses exceed its gains.

The writer was Aldo Leopold, one of the inspiring saints of contemporary environmentalism. He was also, before it was published in 1941, a consultant to the WPA Writers' Program *Wisconsin: A Guide to the Badger State*, whose research editor, living in Madison at the time, was Lorine Niedecker.

Speculations are always hard to resist, but nobody needs to propose a biographical connection when the attitudes are in print themselves. The excerpts from Niedecker's letter and Leopold's article imply, whatever their immediate genesis, a shared, recognizable desire for a wealth where, as Whitman so perfectly put it, every atom belonging to me as good belongs to you—and you don't have to be clear whether the atom is currently in the biota or not. Both excerpts imply a recognizable faith in a commonwealth whose abiding satisfactions might rest in the irrepressible transit of earth into life and back again. This is indeed what Emerson was getting at. In the awesome last paragraph of "Nature" (the great essay, not *Nature* the book), Emerson invoked the popular idea of the sublime, the doctrine of the immortality of the soul, in order to replace it with the sublimer reality of the evolving earth. "The reality," he says there with stunning concision, "is more excellent than the report." It is a concision "Lake Superior" seems ready to confirm.

II

Desire can hardly be the lengthened invention of one individual, not even Emerson. There must be some persistent urgency that makes poems like "Lake Superior" recurrently useful to a certain strain of American psyche. Harold Bloom has described how poems emerge from the struggle with their precursor poems, poets from poets. In that New World where the poet's subject is the commonwealth, I think there are other precursors who raise as provocative an anxiety. These are the discoverers. One sign of how much anxiety they provoke is that we know better than to call them discoverers and are up and willing, centuries after the fact, to take sides over whether they were malevolent predators or just evil ones. In terms of the poetic tradition, though, they were unarguably and unforgivably first: first to relate on the record their apprisals of the commonwealth, of Lake Superior, as in the process its riches were betrayed.

Niedecker began to write her own "Lake Superior" in 1966, following a summer vacation with her husband, Albert Millen, that took them in his Buick from Milwaukee to Green Bay, up Lake Michigan's northern shoulder to St. Ignace, from Sault Ste. Marie westward around the north shore of Lake Superior, and on into the northern Minnesota lake country where Millen had been born and raised and where the Mississippi has its source. The notes Niedecker made during and after this trip have survived. They were brought to my attention by Jenny Penberthy, and for permission to quote them I am grateful to Gail and Bonnie Roub, the neighbors who preserved them, and to Cid Corman, literary executor of Niedecker's estate. The notes (some thirty pages) refer not only to the geology of the vast area that Niedecker and her husband crossed ("Traverse des Millens!" she once called it), but also, and extensively, to the precursor explorers who got to map it first. This is more than a figure of speech. The Jesuit missionary explorers, "black robes" like Jacques Marquette, did in fact make the earliest accurate maps of the Great Lakes, including a famous one from around 1680

> Through all this granite land
> the sign of the cross

which is first to represent the upper Mississippi, and on which the mission sites are marked, as is granite on geological maps today, by crosses.

But notes or no, it would be wrong to imagine that the figures named in Niedecker's poem are so recondite that she or her compatriot reader should need an encyclopedia to be aware of their historical significance. Radisson, most famous of *coureurs de bois*, was in his late twenties when he and Gro-seilliers became, in the words of the old *Wisconsin* guide, the "first white men to penetrate beyond the Great Lakes" into Wisconsin and Minnesota: they were to be remembered in classrooms there as Radishes and Goose-berries. Marquette was thirty-six when he left his mission at St. Ignace and went with twenty-eight-year-old Joliet to look for the Mississippi: his me-morials include a mural in the Milwaukee Public Museum that depicts him standing in his canoe, face upturned and hands aloft in devotion as three converts paddle him to destiny. Even Schoolcraft, mineralogist, ethnographer and US Indian Agent, twenty-seven when he made the journey most likely referred to in the poem, is no stranger: his pioneer if misguided ethnographies led Longfellow to place an Iroquois hero, Hiawatha, forever in the Lake Superior territory of the Ojibwa enemy, a taunt that survives in countless reminders including, in Schoolcraft County, the Hiawatha National Forest that Niedecker and her husband drove through as they proceeded into Upper Michigan and on toward Schoolcraft's agency house, still standing, in Sault Ste. Marie.

Those are Niedecker's precursor explorers, and it is probably no surprise that she has named the ones whose journeys, taken together, just about circumnavigate her native Wisconsin. No surprise, either, if their journeys have in common that each was first to open Wisconsin and the surrounding region to yet another kind of plunder: furs, lead, copper, iron, souls, and ethnographic pelf. It is all a fascination and it is all grotesque. In the names of counties, forests, towns, at markers along the road and monuments in the parks, you walk in on a kind of Primal Scene, the transgression by which you were engendered, and nobody tells you to look the other way. In Wyalusing State Park in Wisconsin, where Niedecker and Millen stopped on an earlier trip in 1963, there is even a monument to that very symbol of extinguished commonwealth

Did not man . . .

mash the cobalt
and carnelian
of that bird

the passenger pigeon. Anywhere in North America, the anxiety of this kind of influence must be broadly the same. Beautiful as the land still is, and mine, it should not have happened this way. As far as the commonwealth is concerned, every one of us must know it would be better if we had never arrived.

Along with the contrition, however, goes the complicity, because who wouldn't want that adventure, to stand there first, to look on eden with a wild surmise? "We weare Cesars," wrote Radisson, "being nobody to contradict us." In this regard I think it is fair to say that Niedecker associated the lingering wildness of Lake Superior with a desire for unopposed poetic immortality. She gives herself away in a letter to Gail Roub, the neighbor who took what is perhaps the most memorable photograph of her, home at Blackhawk Island on the Rock River, her house out of sight on shore in the background. Niedecker was afraid his photo was too candid, not enough like those of Cather and Dickinson which were, she wrote him, "perfectly calm & beautiful—they belong with Time, you might say." Then without a pause she added: "There are some timeless, smooth rocks up around L. Superior. Schoolcraft, by the way, called that lake 'the blue profound.'" It is a totally believable association, especially when you remember how Whitman invoked his bards of the future also on a great lake, not by Superior's but by blue Ontario's shore. Then as now, the problem for a bard of the commonwealth was this: you have to believe your country wants you, just as it spurs desire if your partner feels it too. Like Radisson, you have to believe there is nobody to contradict you.

When the contradictions are strong as the desire, the only way out is the sublime. This is the escape route to poetry that today's readers may recognize better as repression, followed by emergence into a language where, from then on, you are on your own. Intuitively, you might suspect that a procedure that helps to deal with literary origins could help with the origins I have been suggesting as well. The evidence to support the intuition is right there in "Lake Superior," as Niedecker removes her precursor explorers one by one from the land and identifies her hopes for her unconscious directly with the geology itself. We also have her own testimony as it appears in her vacation notes, just after she has described the eons-long itinerary of a pebble in this Lakes country that, after the lava and before the glacier, was once covered by a sea.

> The sea went over and left me dry, parched for knowledge! The feeling of being a part of all this. How?—the body, the unconscious. Let us sing, as they say in church.

Later there was still further evidence of Niedecker's unspoken designs on her discovering predecessors, and on the priestliest of them too. When she first finished "Lake Superior," in October 1966, it did not yet include the section on Marquette. That was a separate poem. Not for another year would she decide to bury Marquette in *her* Lake Superior, over which she, not he, has risen. In the month when she must have been making this decision Niedecker wrote to Cid Corman, reported a visit to Wisconsin's Door Peninsula, and perhaps unknowingly signaled her motives in what now seem the least controvertible of terms. "The whole north country, I'm completely absorbed in it, I'm buried and rise again!"

A redemptory intent like Niedecker's shows up in much of American art. Today it erupts frequently into environmentalist prose, with results that are sometimes lamented as the nature writer's one note, Wonder. But scoffing is easy, and wonder is only the spell the writer casts in an attempt to transform loss into some kind of enduringly positive sustenance. In 1947, when that monument to the lost passenger pigeon was dedicated in Wyalusing State Park, the occasion was commemorated by another article from Aldo Leopold —this one too in *A Sand County Almanac*.

> For one species to mourn the death of another is a new thing under the sun. . . . To see America as history, to conceive of destiny as a becoming, to smell a hickory tree through the still lapse of ages—all these things are possible for us, and to achieve them takes only the free sky, and the will to ply our wings.

35

Redemption, it needs to be said, is not the same as nostalgia. When it is desired by one species for the others, or for the land as a whole, it really is something new under the sun. Perhaps it is the one cultural achievement, though the price was dear, that might be the glory yet of human presence: a passionate deference to the organic and inorganic commonwealth that cannot otherwise speak for itself. In the meantime, and as demonstrated once more by Niedecker in "Lake Superior," this same deference has already become the identifiable, continuing attitude of the tradition we might call not the egotistical, but the evolutional sublime.

III

Attitude takes style, and a likely style if you are reaching for the sublime is hyperbole, or exaggeration. The Aldo Leopold quotation is an example of hyperbole. Sometimes, though, the sublime seems better served by hyperbole's mirror image, abbreviation, or litotes. This was the choice posed so movingly at the beginning of John Ashbery's *Three Poems*.

> I thought if I could put it all down, that would be one way. And next the thought came to me that to leave all out would be another, and truer, way.

Niedecker, as we know, chose leaving out. In all of "Lake Superior" there are but 393 words, and for that you have to include (as readers should) the subtitles. The paradox is how much the poem gets in by leaving out.

The impulse to concision must strike some readers as an impairment. Based on Niedecker's example, I would sooner argue that "leaving out" is the freedom you fight for when you can no longer bear the received deceit of the sentence, the connectives and prepositions that accumulate with the weight of irredeemably inaccurate history. One strategy is to go ahead and employ all the syntax of the sentence while staving off disgust with a strong dose of irony. This will cease to work, however, if you have come to fear irony as just one more accent of fraud in the prison house of prose. In that case the sentence becomes a temptation to avoid, a temptation I think Niedecker acknowledged as her own when she made her otherwise too famous comment, in a letter of 1968, "Koch, Ashbery—there but for the grace of God and Louis Zukofsky go I."

Niedecker's response to the sentence, at its most pronounced in "Lake Superior," was to scour the sentence as if to sand, the way the glacier scoured the Lake Superior rocks. Her style became in this way a cognate for the evolutional attitude: primal elements in evolving arrangements. Even words, since as proofreader at *Hoard's Dairyman* she worked for six years in what she once called a "print shop" where agate (which is also a color, iron-oxide red) might mean a size of type

in my mind

between my toes

agate

even words are a kind of sand. Words are for rearrangement, much as the history of Lake Superior has been the evolutionary rearrangement of its minerals by lava, sea, glacier and human industry: the whole Lakes Basin being in this way a kind of sand lake. Thus the poet never misses Sand Lake

I'm sorry to have missed

Sand Lake

My dear one tells me

we did not

We watched a gopher there

because she is an example of it. As are we all, who, following the land treaty at Prairie du Chien in 1825, moved like a boom of gophers to dig, mine and rearrange the earth all over Wisconsin and (the gopher state) Minnesota.

Niedecker's own rearrangements have redemptive ends. If you treat words like sand, stories by their constituent elements, perhaps you can incorporate the contradictions that created you, embody them enough to leave the land clean again on its surface for desire. Of this hope there is no more resonant example than the Radisson section of "Lake Superior."

Radisson:

'a laborinth of pleasure'
this world of the Lake

Long hair, long gun

Fingernails pulled out
by Mohawks

(The long

canoes)

The reviewer I mentioned at the outset (it was Donald Davie) read this section as only potentially pathetic, an attempt to win for Radisson a pity that, as predator in someone else's land, he did not deserve. And yet Radisson's fingernails were extracted during an eighteen-month captivity that began in 1652 when he was taken, as we would say, *hostage* from the outskirts of Trois Rivières, in Quebec, where he lived. He was at most twenty. Seven years elapsed before he and Groseilliers would first penetrate into the Wisconsin country he called "a laborinth of pleasure," and another nine or ten before, in England in 1668–9, he wrote those words themselves. Niedecker has reversed the chronology. She has reversed it as if to insist on the preeminence of desire. Knowing for certain of pain, her Radisson speaks first, speaks only, of pleasure. Without thought of pity he speaks, through her arrangement, of the wonder of desire for the dominant X of earth.

There was more. Radisson and Groseilliers astonished Quebec by returning from their Lake Superior voyage at the head of 360 long canoes—the parentheses make (the long canoes) even look like downriver canoes—so laden with furs that they saved the economy of New France. The two were fined, the furs were confiscated, Groseilliers was jailed. They had gone without a permit. Nor would Paris take seriously their discovery that Hudson Bay could provide a better route for the fur trade. Unrepentant, the partners tendered their new expertise to London

Gulls playing both sides

and, fatefully for New France, the Hudson's Bay Company was born. There would be further instances too of Radisson gulling and being gulled by rival sides. Still he speaks only of pleasure. The wonder of desire for the country is how it supersedes the state. The wonder of Niedecker's style is how this "discoverer" now discovers our wisdom and follows, none to contradict him, our desire.

Although "Lake Superior" may at first seem spare of words, Niedecker can be wide and generous within a single one of them. Sometimes she practically harmonizes with herself. Readers who recall her lines from another poem about "the very veery"

> We are what the seas
> have made us
>
> longingly immense
>
> the very veery
> on the fence

may know where I got that idea. The veery is a thrush that actually does sing in harmony with itself. A bird's syrinx is capable of more than one note at a time, and the veery takes advantage of its ability to produce an unusually allusive, yet one "word," song. An example of like effect in "Lake Superior"

39

occurs in Niedecker's description of the Schoolcraft expedition, as it proceeded west along the south shore to old Fond du Lac at the end of the lake, and on into

> the redolent pondy lakes

of northern Minnesota. Schoolcraft made his first such trip in 1820 as the Americans belatedly arrived, flags flying, to take possession of the area. He went along as mineralogist. But anybody who reasons by syllables, and who knows how carefully Niedecker avoids redundant ones, might hear in the syllables I just quoted a reminder that in another six years Schoolcraft will make the trip again, as US Indian Agent this time, to oversee the treaty of

> pon dy lakes
> fond du lac

Fond du Lac by which the Ojibwa will sign over "the right to search for, and carry away, any metals or minerals from any part of their country"

> Iron the common element of earth

to the United States. In one widening note, Niedecker avoids the monotony of wonder and has harmonized wonder with its human cost. She has been like the veery, immensely concise.

IV

Whitman told us that the effect of true poets was to bring people back from their sickly abstractions to the divine, original concrete. From the moment I discovered "Lake Superior" I thought it just right, therefore, that Niedecker went for her material directly to the place she calls in the poem "true source park." It seemed an especially skillful phrase for the divine, original concrete outside the human voice, except it was even more skillful than that. Niedecker was singing two notes at once again. Her "true source park" turns out also to mean its opposite, the literary source—the human source, for that matter—of reality.

When Schoolcraft finally located the pondy lake in Minnesota that he believed to be the source of the Mississippi River he named, or rather renamed it Lake Itasca. The word Itasca is not Ojibwa or Dakota, the two contenders for an indigenous naming. It is a neologism invented by Henry Rowe Schoolcraft from the three middle syllables of *veritas caput*, signifying true source. Millions of tourists have now walked across the Mississippi without getting their feet wet at, inevitably, Itasca State Park. Niedecker and Millen stopped there in 1966 after having driven on from Lake Superior. It is all a fascination, it is grotesque, and sometimes it is a kind of farce. At roadside markers, in parks, you stumble in on the inventive transgressions by which you were engendered—*veritas caput*, can you believe?—and nobody tells you to look the other way. Surely Niedecker must have meant the true true source: rocks, minerals, gneiss. Just as surely she meant also that there is a deception at the very fundament of true source park, and the deception is language, literature.

Sweet deception. Throughout "Lake Superior" runs like a canoe the shadow of Schoolcraft's unexpected progeny, *The Song of Hiawatha*. The first poem I remember hearing (in my grandmother's voice) was *Hiawatha*, and hearing it like that how could anybody forget the insistence of it?

> By the shores of Gitche Gumee
> By the shining Big Sea Water

Today I know of course that Longfellow, drawing chiefly on Schoolcraft's *Algic Researches* and multivolume ethnography, was drawing on material in some cases about as indigenous as the word Itasca. I know Longfellow even compounded the iniquity

Beauty: impurities in the rock

by adding willful misrepresentations of his own. The question is whether to be indignant over the cultural impurities that have preceded us onto the land or to think of them as, of all things, beauty.

The slightly paradoxical answer of "Lake Superior" seems to be that literature is beauty as long as it leads you to true source park, and back. People forget, in their fresh indignation against Longfellow, the function *Hiawatha* itself once performed. It led imaginations inland, away from sickly abstractions to the lakes and woods. (It was among Aldo Leopold's favorite books even at Yale.) In fact the South Shore journey

> as if Life's—

that has been really repressed in "Lake Superior" is Hiawatha's. If you were another Harold Bloom you might be justly gratified to point out that Hiawatha's first quest westward along the shores of the lake was to locate and defeat his own precursor, his father. In the ensuing struggle, the weapon Hiawatha picks up

> The smooth black stone
> I picked up in true source park

is fatal Wawbeek, the black rock. The battle will end as a draw, but what hasn't ended yet is the task Hiawatha took up on the spot, given him in his father's words.

> "Go back to your home and people,
> Live among them, toil among them,
> Cleanse the earth from all that harms it,
> Clear the fishing-grounds and rivers,
> Slay the monsters and magicians. . . ."

Now that I'm grown and know how to cringe I can admit that this thrilling passage was grade B property at best. But to the extent it reveals Longfellow's motives (he sounds like an emerging eco-activist, his Hiawatha a Greenpeace warrior), he wasn't such a drip after all. Besides, what if you could convince him of his errors? He is unlikely to fix them now.

The only way to cleanse the earth of the old *Hiawatha* is to write a new one. The point isn't whether Niedecker knew Lake Superior was the shining Big Sea Water, though of course she did. The point is she knew we would know. Given the allusive concision of her style, she would never have to bring this knowledge to the surface. Treating words like sand, she could return the literature of Lake Superior to its constituent physics in which every atom belonging to me, belongs to you. In "Lake Superior" you can almost feel the land *wanting* you again, feel the reciprocal desire to make poetry

> The smooth black stone
> I picked up in true source park
> the leaf beside it
> once was stone

from unmediated contact with matter. Emerson thought poetry a kind of second nature, like a "leaf," he wrote, from a tree, and the first great poems to follow his lead were of course called "Leaves." So the leaf that once was stone in "Lake Superior" is, in Niedecker's litotic harmony, also a poem. Reduce your precursor errors to their constituent elements, and poems can be made again, not of words, but stone.

v

In a land where poems are made of stone, and rock, there could be no more stupendous region for Niedecker to visit than the Lake Superior country where uplift and glacier have exposed the oldest rock on earth. A great knob of this rock that was "superior" in strength to the ice

> And at the blue ice superior spot
> priest-robed Marquette grazed
> azoic rock

rises west of the town named for Marquette on the lake's south shore, a result of the Laurentian orogeny that formed the granite of the Canadian Shield three billion years ago. The north shore is all such granite. In the whole Lakes country the glacier left no rock that is not at least 280 million years old. It is a place to sense evolution at its most powerfully telescoped. Even the fossil record is gone, scoured off by the glacier. You stand on trilobites. Iron was discovered on the Marquette Range in 1844, almost pure, among the last elements to have been manufactured in some anciently distant star before it shed its mineral wealth into space, and set the course for eventual human contact along *le lac supèrieur*.

It's no wonder, in such a country, if *"voyageurs* crossed themselves" and "Chippewas threw deermeat," and no wonder either if a poet in the tradition of the evolutional sublime

> Why should we hurry
> home

should feel strangely at home. ("Maybe as rocks and I pass each other I could say how-do-you-do to an agate," noted Niedecker as her trip began.) In the essay "Nature," Emerson seems already to have described the place.

> We come to our own, and make friends with matter, which the ambitious chatter of the schools would persuade us to despise. We can never part with it; the mind loves its old home: as water to our thirst, so is rock, the ground, to our eyes, and hands, and feet. It is firm water: it is cold flame: what health, what affinity!

From the mind's old home there would be scant reason to hurry back to a world so predictably inferior.

On the other hand, if inanimate matter equals stony rest then there's no reason to hurry to that home, either, or hurry it along, not when we are so desirably lively now. Of course life is not good enough for everyone, I know. Critics who find the evolutional tradition alien seem largely to be repelled because it doesn't provide immortality (or is it the discipline of damnation they miss?) for the individual soul. The pique is more evident if they are criticizing not Emerson or Whitman, but an easier target like Robinson Jeffers, and can disguise their animus as taste. Yet the poets in this tradition will continue by definition to apprise us of a commonwealth that is indeed without revelation. In North America, nature has revealed no special exemptions for the human race, no single truth. The continent itself is True Source Park. Or as Emerson responded in exasperation when someone tried to settle an argument by citing the other world, "Other world? there is no other world; here or nowhere is the whole fact."

Niedecker's deft gift to this tradition is that she will not let her excursion into its sublime end in mere grandeur. She offers her poem, but on the condition apparently that the sublime make room for her own disabused tenderness toward the most expensive, precarious component of evolution, the human one. The Sand Lake she missed in "Lake Superior," or didn't, is a case in point. It is not the lake in Ontario identified in the *Norton Anthology*. The *Norton* took her spelling too literally and forgot how ruthless Niedecker can be with an unwanted syllable. Sand(y) Lake, as the westering itinerary of the poem itself implies, is in Minnesota, the site of the Sandy Lake trading post where in late 1850 the Ojibwa bands of Wisconsin were directed to receive their annuities. The United States had already ordered the Wisconsin Ojibwa permanently removed to Minnesota, and now the idea was to delay distribution of their annuities until the increasingly bitter winter would force them to remain. As many as four hundred died near Sandy Lake or

> Why should we hurry
>
> home

trying to walk home, back into Wisconsin. A hundred years had passed since the once expansionist Ojibwa had forced the Dakota to evacuate a village of their own at Sandy Lake.

To a man, the explorers who preceded Niedecker at Lake Superior had treated the land as theirs for the taking. Radisson didn't call it a laborinth of pleasure for nothing. A modernized version of his *Voyages* gives you an idea of what he had in mind. "What conquest would that be at little or no cost, what labyrinth of pleasure should millions of people have, instead that millions complain of misery and poverty?" In a sense the land took Radisson, as agent, instead. His very name, Pierre, means stone. Orimha, his adopted Mohawk name, meant stone. Marquette sought to raise souls up to life everlasting, made contact instead with prelifeform (azoic) rock and, after his converts in homage carved the unresurrected meat from his bones, was born again in the name of the Marquette Range as iron ore, rock. Schoolcraft couldn't believe nature had created such a scene of magnificence, as he put it in his *Memoirs*, "merely to look at." A mineralogist tapping away with his hammer, he was known to the Ojibwa as Paw-gwa-be-ca-we-ga, Destroyer of Rocks, which reveals on their part a certain prospective irony since Schoolcraft is gone and rocks are still here. Anxious to extract the wealth and take it "home," Niedecker's predecessors never got the news

> Why should we hurry

that this is home—iron in our blood, a transit of minerals ourselves, and necessarily native in the larger transit "Lake Superior" will describe in accents of the evolutional sublime.

By the time Niedecker and her husband made their trip around great *Kitchigami*, in 1966, it seemed clear that the once invasive American population would continue to treat its commonwealth with no letup of contempt. "Often on the trip the stones that had a shine turned out to be bottlecaps," reports Niedecker in her notes. On the Minnesota shore, at the first port south of Gooseberry (nè Groseilliers) Falls, the Western Reserve Mining Company was into its eleventh year of shedding slag straight into the lake, a rapture of industrial vandalism that wouldn't end until 1980. As a direct result, the western floor of "the blue profound" is covered today in asbestos sludge—and I think anyone who reflects on the severity and permanence of such violence might justifiably demand to know how it could happen in a land where the evolutional sublime is the tradition I have been making it out to be. The patient, unworn answer is that in this species we die miserably every year for lack of the news we could find in poetry. And the news in American poetry has yet to reach people who still, against all available evidence, regard humans, not rocks, as the heroes of this earth.

The more intimate question posed by "Lake Superior" is whether the news is at an end. Can an evolutional earth ethic help an urban population to fashion human selves and achieve human connectedness in a time tectonic with cultures, and commerce, and claims? Offered multiple panoramas on tape, in travel, on film, who really could care about pebbles, orogenies, stone? Maybe it's too obvious to say. In such a time, more especially in such a place, the land is the one thing that people who can't afford vacations in Europe do have in common. When Niedecker retells in "Lake Superior" the story of Joliet, ex-priest, fur-trader, adventurer, native Quebecois

> At Hudson Bay he conversed in latin
> with an Englishman

she projects our necessary cultural dexterity as if to say, the new world has always been like this. When she represents the figure who proceeded onto the austere lake

> Schoolcraft left the Soo—canoes
> US pennants, masts, sails
> chanting canoemen, barge
> soldiers—for Minnesota

like a spectacle out of Hollywood, bearing blandishments of the sort the White House basement might devise, she projects our image-daft innocence as if to say, the new world was always like this.

Niedecker liked language and she was fond of the corruptions that might make it momentarily, transitionally indigenous. Soo, for example, is the funny way Michiganders say Sault (as in Soo Saint MuhREE), but the pronunciation was made deeply serious when applied to the strategic Soo canal. "The North is one vast, massive, glorious corruption of rock and language," observes Niedecker in her notes. "People of all nationalities and color have changed the language like weather and pressure have changed the rocks." She enjoyed the story she recounted in a letter to Corman of how Schoolcraft on expedition was greeted from shore with shouts of "bosho!"—a noise made locally to signify *bonjour*. Read it against such rich corruptions, and Niedecker's "Lake Superior" seems all the more in profound contrast. Her style seems by its immense concision to say what her subject matter likewise says, that on this linguistically promiscuous and overwhelmingly talkative continent the self will not be composed of language only. It is also composed

> wave-washed and the rains
> did their work and a green
> running as from copper

of the mute things we look upon, the unspoke beauty of them. Desire may even equal just that percentage of things we feel as yet to be unspoke. And that true source, where every atom belonging to me as good as belongs to you, is perhaps the one ultimate connectedness at last possible for the democratic individual.

Wordsworth, in the 1802 Preface, used the word *human* eleven times, each time favorably. Emerson, in "The Poet," used it only once, and then to denote a limitation to be escaped. Poets, he wrote, must unlock at all risks their "human doors" and be caught up instead into the life and thought of the universe. "Man is made of the same atoms the world is," he would write in a later essay. "When his mind is illuminated, when his heart is kind, he throws himself joyfully into the sublime order, and does, with knowledge, what the stones do by structure." So Aldo Leopold was securely in the tradition when he introduced into our ethics a phrase that has become almost scriptural: thinking like a mountain. Niedecker in turn could coax you into thinking like Lake Superior. On Lake Superior not one human culture exactly fits. Maybe none ever will. In the meantime the promise of Niedecker's brave pastoral is that the poetry of the evolutional sublime will continue to arrive, bringing its news, to set desire free for a wealth that is yours

> Inland then
> beside the great granite
> gneiss and the schists

clean through to the oldest rocks in the world. There, thinking like Lake Superior, you might even regard it the least repellent, most promising of poetries that could realize rock as the last "laborinth of pleasure" humans have got. Pleasure: because, as Wordsworth said, humans have no sympathy but what is propagated by that.

Three Letters from Lorine Niedecker to Cid Corman

Dear Cid:

Setting off by auto for Lake Superior by way of L. Mich. shore to Mackinaw Country and Sault Ste. Marie. The road goes along the Ontario shore and down the Minn. side. Al's vacation.

Please get some kind of good out of the $10 enclosed.

J.W. says T & G (Tenderness and Gristle) will be out by January, "a small but very fine press in N.Y."—had I told you before what the name of my book is? I owe it to Lawrence Durrell, not that I read him very much. I read few novels.

Hot here, almost unbearable. The clear cool air of the north might take me sinus infection away.

Yours
Lorine

Stuart Montgomery sent Gary Snyder's "A Range of Poems"—I'm interested. So far I have 2 Origins (July) May I have 2 more or at least one more?

Dear Cid:

The Snyder book—meant to say the drawings by Will Petersen exactly, delightfully suit the poetry, I think.

You once spoke to me of rocks—someone there, is it Will Petersen?—has an interest in them. I begin to see how one can have. I think our NW (Lake Superior region, Minn., Mich., Wis.) is not only for the geologist, a massive, grand corruption of nature. And of language (wonder if *Bosho* is still used in speech for *Bon jour!* Indian, French, British—. The Northwest passage to the Orient has its Bosho only like a ton of rock. And weak verse like Longfellow's *Hiawatha*. But some kind of poetry has been felt by several of the geologists in that region.

I'm frantic when I remember that gold and diamond ! driveway in South Dakota, not knowing what kind of stone or mineral it was. Probably a lot of quartz in it to give the shine.

I'll use a little time to walk beaches since this country is part of the agate, jasper, carnelian, Thompsonite region. I can't buy an agate because I have read that agates can be commercially dyed. Al suggests that possibly the rock shops even up that way (L. S.) could be stocked with stones "made in Japan"! The [curio, area] gift shops are our modern day Passage to the Orient.

Cid, no, I won't be writing for awhile, and I need time, like an eon of limestone or gneiss, time like I used to have, with no *thought* of publishing. I'm very slow anyhow, you know. So if you don't receive any poems from me for a long time, please understand. And I feel that nothing of my letters should be published. You speak of transcriptions—from my letters?—I'd rather not—but perhaps you mean mention of the July Origin by persons writing you, oh of course let me know what the reaction is "out there."

Ian has a son, it seems! And a Sue (the child's mother, I take it.) A word from him—living at this time a comparatively sane life, it seems. Asks me to make up an LN issue of POTH—I declined.

Briggflatts won't get here (Poetry) before we go but we'll be back Aug. 1.

Strange—we are always inhabiting more than one realm of existence—but they all fit in if the art is right.

———Best to you
both———
Lorine

Dear Cid:

The Eshleman criticism—well, I know—and as you say—! I suppose it's called the balance of (poetic) nature—I read both Eshleman and Enslin everywhere I can, usually looking up to them. Funny thing—I have in my special notebook where few poems get put two of Eshleman's which I suppose represent his mystical tendency but so exactly as a poet "thinks" but seldom dares to let out into print—

One Morning

That I not over-
simplify contour,
the maple

the sky

———————

I am taking a walk holding Barbara's
hand, a field
slower than centuries we've no mind of

———

I believe they were in an *Origin?*

However, I think you could feel in my last letter or the one before that,

52

I'm going into a kind of retreat so far as time (going to be geologic time from now on!) is concerned because a lot of it without being printed much is always on my side. I can no longer accommodate the periodicals that want a sizeable amount of work from me. But they write me asking to feature—I can't, I'm all caught up, the book is coming out, no one should mind since the few that will appear sometime in the future should be good.

Geologic—I wish your friend Ohno were here—sending stones costs, they weigh up. Thank you for Will Petersen's address. I think, tho, I'll run into a geologist here some day and I've sent for geological maps from the office in Washington, D.C. As for semiprecious ones, I bought at little or nothing while on the trip a Lake Superior agate, a carnelian (o that color) from Uruguay and a sodilite from Canada. Just to run the finger over the polished gleaming color. Thin circling lines in the agate with a rather wide orange band. Seems petrified wood and agate have a connection—almost all petrified wood is agate-ized wood, I've read. The circles in the agate are of growth? Dunno, aim to find out.

And, I meant to say re Eshleman there he is printing your *At: Bottom*, that most beautiful prose—absolutely lovely, Cid, as lovely as the book. I must put it with *for instance* and Walden and Lucretius and LZ etc. in my cupboard corner.

Yes, the Lake Superior trip was a great delight if I can make the poem. Traverse des Millens! A millenium of notes for my *magma* opus!

Before I forget, in addition to those you mentioned that LZ preferred of mine, there is Sewing a dress which he pointed out on a card to me. No accounting for anything, Cid. He names exactly the ones (outside of 1st stanza of the last: "The eye") I never expected he would.

> I see this is going to take
> another aerogramme—
> so number II coming up.

53

FROM

Back Roads to Far Towns

BASHŌ, 1689

(TRANS. CID CORMAN AND KAMAIKE SUSUMU)

1

Moon & sun are passing figures of countless generations, and years coming or going wanderers too. Drifting life away on a boat or meeting age leading a horse by the mouth, each day is a journey and the journey itself home. Amongst those of old were many that perished upon the journey. So—when was it—I, drawn like blown cloud, couldnt stop dreaming of roaming, roving the coast up and down, back at the hut last fall by the river side, sweeping cobwebs off, a year gone and misty skies of spring returning, yearning to go over the Shirakawa Barrier, possessed by the wanderlust, at wits' end, beckoned by Dōsojin, hardly able to keep my hand to any thing, mending a rip in my *momohiki*, replacing the cords in my *kasa*, shins no sooner burnt with

54

moxa than the moon at Matsushima rose to mind and how, my former dwelling passed on to someone else on moving to Sampū's summer house,

> the grass door too
> turning into
> a dolls' house

(from the eight *omote*) set on a post of the hut.

2

Yayoi: last seventh, slightly hazy dawn, "a waning moon, a failing light," summit of Fuji vague, crowns of blossoming cherry at Ueno and Yanaka, when would they—and would they—be seen again? Friends, gathering since nightfall, came along by boat to see us off. Landed at Senju, sense of three thousand *li* ahead swelling the heart, world so much a dream, tears at point of departure.

> departing spring (ya
> birds cry fishes'
> eyes tears

the *yatate*'s first words, the path taken looked not to advance at all. Those filling the way behind watched till only shadows of backs seemed seen.

3

This year, the second—is it—of the Genroku, far only to think how far it is to Ōu "under Go skies," to picture hair turning white, places ears had heard of eyes never seen, likelihood of returning not so bright, just did make the post town of Sōka by nightfall. Thin shoulders feeling packs drag. Body enough, but burdened with a set of *kamiko* (extra protection at night), *yukata*, raincoat, ink-stick, brushes, as well as unavoidable *hanamuke*, etc., somehow hard to let go of, part of the trouble in travelling inevitably.

4

Visited the Muro-no-Yashima. My companion, Sora, said: "The deity here, Konohana Sakuya Hime, is the same as that at Fuji. She went and set fire to the Utsu-muro to prove her innocence and out of this was Prince Hohodemi born and the place called Muro-no-Yashima. And why poetry written about it mentions smoke." Also fish known as *konoshiro* prohibited here. Story behind it common knowledge.

5

Thirtieth. Stayed at foot of Mt. Nikkō. Hosteler says: "They call me Hotoke Gozaemon. Honesty's a habit with me, which is why the name, so feel right to home," what he said. Impossible not to realize how Buddha appears upon this mean and muddled ground in just such guise to help shaman beggar pilgrims on, seeing our host's simple sincere manner, frank and down-to-earth. Firm-grained and unassuming, the very image of the man of *jen*, worthy of all respect.

6

First of Uzuki, called on the mountain shrine. Originally this mountain known as Futarayama, but when Kūkai Daishi dedicated the shrine here, he renamed it Nikkō. Perhaps with presentiment those thousand years ago of the splendor now gracing our skies and the blessings extended to the eight directions to the four classes of citizens living in peace. But with glory so full, so empty are words.

> O glorious
> green leaves young leaves'
> sun light

7

Mt Kurokami hung with mist and still snow clad.

> head shaven
> at Mt Kurokami
> changing apparel
>
> (Sora)

Sora formerly Kawai Sōgorō. In *bashō* shade, eave to eave, helped at wood and water chores. Delighted at the chance to share prospects of Matsushima

57

and Kisakata, offered to take on whatever tasks the journey would call for, at dawn of the day of departure had head shaven, assumed pilgrim garb and signalled the new life by changing name to Sōgo. And so, the Mt Kurokami poem. The words "changing apparel" weigh tellingly.

Climbed more than twenty *chō* uphill to find the waterfall. Plunges from over cavern a hundred *shaku* down to thousand-rock-studded basin below. Stooped into cavern to peer out from behind cascade known as Urami Falls.

> for a while
> to a waterfall confined
> summer opening

Tour 14A

FROM WISCONSIN: A GUIDE TO
THE BADGER STATE (WPA, 1941)

Ashland—Bayfield—Superior, 107.9 *m.*; State 13.

> Oiled-gravel or asphalt roadbed.
>
> Accommodations adequate. Good hotel and restaurant facilities at Bayfield and Washburn.

State 13, alternate route between Ashland and Superior, is almost 40 miles longer than US 2. Curving along the rocky shores of Lake Superior, it passes storm-beaten fishing villages, touches the Red Cliff Indian Reservation, and provides access to the Apostle Islands with their wave-carved cliffs and arches.

ASHLAND, 0 *m.* (666 alt., 10,622 pop.) (*see Tour 8*), is at the junction with US 2 (*see Tour 14*), US 63 (*see Tour 9*), and lower State 13 (*see Tour 8*). Passing grimy coal docks and the steam plant of the Lake Superior District Power Company, the highway rounds the head of Chequamegon Bay and ascends the steep ridge along its western shore.

WASHBURN, 11 *m.* (656 alt., 2,238 pop.), seat of Bayfield County, rises in tiers on the slope of a bluff. Many of its buildings, notably the courthouse, are constructed of reddish-brown stone quarried on Basswood Island (*see below*). Until 1883 not a tree had been cut in this district. In that year the Chicago, St. Paul, Minnesota & Omaha R. R. purchased this site and in 1884 founded a village named for Cadwallader C. Washburn, State Governor (1872–74). Within five years coal docks lined the bayshore, and a freight warehouse, an elevator, and three lumber mills were operating. In Washburn the MOQUAH RANGER STATION (*open to visitors*) guards the cutover.

North of Washburn are faded farmsteads. State 13 descends to the shore of Chequamegon Bay, 14.3 *m.*, and sweeps in a wide curve to densely timbered VAN TASSELL'S POINT, a great hogsback thrusting lakeward. A fire lane cuts straight from the water's edge over the ridge top; quartzite and sandstone shoulder up between the trees. The STATE FISH HATCHERY, 19.9 *m.*, breeds a strain of pure white trout from one- to three-year-old albinos.

BAYFIELD, 22.9 *m.* (617 alt., 1,195 pop.), at the foot of a steep hill, was named for Admiral Henry Bayfield of the British Navy, surveyor of the Great Lakes, who arrived here about 1823. Later, in 1857, nine men under Henry M. Rice of St. Paul arrived and started a village. For a long time Bayfield's only connection with the outside world was by lake and forest trails. Indians, bringing the mail from Superior on foot, required five days for the 85-mile journey; fare for the jolting wagon trip to St. Paul by logging road was $20. About 1880 the railroad came, and the lumbermen took over the region.

On the western outskirts of the city is the BAYFIELD FIRE TOWER, from which the Porcupine Mountains of Michigan, about 30 miles east, appear dimly on the horizon. Scattered in the middle distance are the Apostle Islands (*see below*), a maze of red cliffs, tawny beaches, and channels of cerulean blue, where wisps of smoke drift from the hidden huts of island fisherfolk.

Although trout trolling in Lake Superior has only recently become popular, some 5,000 fishermen now come here annually. (*Boats: $15 to $30 a day including pilot; most boats provide fishing equipment free.*) Fishing is best in the channels between Brownstone (or North Twin) Island, Devils Island, and Bear Island. To catch Lake Superior trout gear equivalent to the strongest muskellunge tackle is required. Heavy silk casting lines will do, though some fishermen insist upon copper or steel lines; large spoon hooks or ordinary casting plugs are adequate as bait. Most fishing is done from cabin cruisers in water 20 to 150 feet deep. Catches range from 5 to 40 pounds. A 35-pound trout, approximately 4 feet long, 10 to 12 inches wide, and 4 to 6 inches thick through the back, will fight desperately until brought to gaff.

The APOSTLE ISLANDS can be visited from Bayfield by an excursion boat (*daily except Sat. bet. July 1 and Sept. 1; leave Bayfield at 10:30 a.m., return at 3:15 p.m.; $1 each person; open for charter*). Fishing boats also take passengers (*$1 each*), and there is a ferry to Madeline Island (*see below*).

Gulls follow the ferry, swoop over the fishing boats, and hover above the cleaning shanties on the islands, which early Frenchmen referred to as the "Twelve Apostles," although there are more than 20 in the group. Most of them rise 20 to 150 feet from the water, and all are being modified by water action.

On Madeline, Michigan, Outer, Devils, Sand, and Raspberry Islands, and at Red Cliff Point on the mainland, are Government lighthouses. Oak, Manitou, Bear, South Twin, and North Twin Islands are inhabited during the summer; Madeline, Stockton, and Sand islands the year round. Wild game is plentiful—deer, mink, muskrat, beaver, otter, wolves, and an occasional bear; thousands of ducks and other migratory waterfowl nest here; and loons, herons, and owls are numerous.

The intricate and grotesque carving of the 10- to 60-foot cliffs have given the Apostle Islands wide fame. On STOCKTON ISLAND are several noteworthy formations: the SPHINX, LONE ROCK, and natural GROTTOS. On the northern point of OAK ISLAND (480 feet alt.) is THE HOLE IN THE WALL, where waves have undermined the entire point and created a natural bridge.

Perhaps the most striking examples of wave erosion are found on DEVILS ISLAND, where in a space of 200 yards there are more than 50 arches, some circular, others Gothic, resting on symmetrical pillars 6 to 12 feet in diameter. The arches overhang SEA CAVES, a few large enough to permit the passage of cabin cruisers. In the subdued light of these subterranean lakes the water is a pale translucent green, lapping gently against the overarching red rocks. There are two well-known formations on this island—TROUT CAVE and DEVILS PIANO.

On SAND ISLAND are the formations of TEMPLE GATE and the THREE-LEGGED STOOL.

HERMIT (Wilson) ISLAND is known for its legendary buried treasure. In the early 1860's a scholarly recluse named Wilson lived here. Because he spent money liberally, it was whispered that he possessed a treasure. After he had been found dead in his cabin, men rushed to the island with shovels and picks, tore up the ground about the cabin, but discovered only a few coins.

Largest and richest in historic associations is MADELINE ISLAND, the only one with roads, villages, and farms. (*Ferry fees: 15¢ one way; 25¢ round trip; car including passengers, $2; leaves Bayfield at 8, 10, and 11 a.m. and 2, 4:30, and 5:30 p.m.; leaves La Pointe at 7 and 9 a.m. and 1, 3, 5, and 7 p.m. Trip takes 20 minutes. Ferry docks at City Dock and Mission Inn Docks on Madeline Island.*)

At the southwestern tip of the island is the settlement of LA POINTE, a name first given to the Jesuit mission established on the mainland by Allouez in 1665. Several years later the name came to signify the entire Chequamegon Bay region; not until 1718, when Fort La Pointe was built here by St. Pierre and Linctot, did the name become closely associated with Madeline Island.

Fort La Pointe was the second French fort on the island; the first, erected by Le Sueur in 1693 and abandoned in 1698, held open the route from Lake Superior to the Mississippi for French trade. Fort La Pointe was established to maintain peace among the Indian tribes in this region. In 1727 Louis Denis, Sieur de la Ronde, was given command of the fort. While La Ronde was in charge, the fort was garrisoned; a dock and probably a mill were built; some agriculture was carried on.

The Indians at La Pointe told the French of an island of copper guarded by spirits; La Ronde, when he heard of the mineral, requested permission from the French Government to combine his duties at the fort with mining. He was not given permission to operate the mines until 1733, and in 1740 his mining activities were halted by an outbreak between the Sioux and the Chippewa. Nonetheless, La Ronde is known as the first practical miner on Lake Superior, and the man who opened this region for settlement by white men.

La Ronde was succeeded by his eldest son, Philippe. In 1749 Joseph Marin was given charge of the fort, which by this time was a subsidiary of a Mississippi river post and had lost much of its importance. In 1759, during the French and Indian War, the French commandant and the garrison were withdrawn.

Alexander Henry, English fur trader, revived trading activity here in 1765. Michel Cadotte built a post near the site of Fort La Pointe about 1800 and strengthened his influence as a trader with the Indians by marrying the daughter of the local Chippewa chief. First an agent of the North West Fur Company and later of Astor's American Fur Company, Cadotte was joined in 1818 by two Warren brothers, who married his half-breed daughters and remained as agents until La Pointe lost its commercial significance.

A PROTESTANT MISSION, built in 1832 near the western end of the island, is still used. Carefully restored, its inner walls are lined with birchbark, cut and fitted as accurately as wallpaper. In 1832 the American Fur Company moved its post to this part of the island. It was here, on the council grounds adjoining the warehouse, that the Chippewa signed the treaty of 1854 that established reservations for each of their separate bands.

RED CLIFF, 25 m., lying in a glade between upland and bay, consists of scattered Indian huts, most of them unpainted. Indian children play and swarthy men loiter in bedraggled yards. The white refer to these Indians as "shiftless bow-and-arrows," but their poverty and shiftlessness is largely owing to the infertility of their land and the allotment of individual holdings (see Tour 15). The INDIAN CATHOLIC CHURCH, 25.9 m., is the cultural center of the community.

The RED CLIFF INDIAN RESERVATION encircles the rounded tip of the Bayfield Peninsula. Here live the descendants of a group of La Pointe Chippewa Indians (see Tour 14), who, given 14,142 acres of land by the treaty of 1854, settled here under the leadership of Chief Buffalo. Only 3,856 acres in the reservation remain in the hands of individual Indians, most of whom have sold their allotments. The Federal Government has purchased 930 acres to add to the reservation. Only a few rough country roads lead into the reservation from State 13. Lake fishing, the support of many coast settlements, is not open to these Indians because of the large amounts of capital required (*see below*). Most of the Indians on the barren reservation live on Government pensions and county relief.

In the reservation, near the mouth of the Sand River, is a DEER YARD, where hundreds of deer winter in the depths of a black spruce swamp. The whole yard reeks with their musky odor. Through the long winter the deer nibble the needles, bark, and twigs of spruce and swamp alder; but toward spring they become weak from hunger, hardly able to fend off the wolves, and fall easy victims to pneumonia. The State Conservation Department hauls hay into the yard, but even so the deer suffer greatly during a hard winter.

State 13 swings west through a gap in the hills and crosses the end of the peninsula. A few shabby farms dot the countryside. Here and there along the roadside is a portable sawmill, cutting boards from larger logs, sawing smaller ones into posts, ties, pulpwood, and cordwood. Cordwood, the principal fuel for both cooking and heating, sells at $1.50 to $2.50 a cord.

At 41 *m.* State 13 runs along the shore of Squaw Bay.

Northeast of this point (*accessible only by boat for rent at Holton Farm*) are some RED CLIFF CAVES, 3 *m.*, and rock formations almost as odd as those of the Apostle Islands. Several of the sea caves are large enough to admit a boat, many of them higher than those on Devils Island. At one point is a great cleft in the rock which goes back into the bluff some 300 feet; its walls rise in an overhanging arch 70 or 80 feet high. The water when quiet is crystal clear, and deep within it fish can be seen swimming in and out of the cove. Ferns and moss grow over the rocks, and mountain ash clings to the sides of the cliffs, its vermilion berries vivid against the green growth and the reddish brown of the stone. Owls nest in pockets of the rock, only their yellow eyes visible; a cautious climber can approach within a few feet of them. Woodchucks, gophers, and chipmunks scurry along the ledges; occasionally a deer appears on the brink of the cliffs.

EAGLE ISLAND, just opposite, was so named because eagles have nested there for years.

CORNUCOPIA, 44.4 *m.*, on Siskowitt Bay at the mouth of the Siskowitt River, is a fishing town. Stiff gray fishing nets hang drying on big reels; weathered shacks crowd to the shore line with its old docks; thousands of gulls flash white against the sky, wheeling and dipping in search of food.

In 1938, 18 fishing boats, from 26-foot cabin cruisers to 60-foot tugs, all equipped with gasoline engines, operated from this base. They range as far as Isle Royale for trout, whitefish, and longjaw, bringing in daily catches of from 300 to 1,000 pounds. The fishermen receive 10¢ to 14¢ pound. When the herring run, a lift of 3 or 4 tons a day is common; a load of 10 tons is not unknown. As herring bring from $30 to $40 a ton, fishermen receive large gross incomes during the season. The investment required for boats, nets, and equipment is high, ranging from $2,500 to $10,000 for each outfit; for 6 months the lake, choked with ice, is unnavigable; and during the remaining 6 months fishing is periodically restricted by conservation laws.

Left from Cornucopia on County C to the FALLS OF THE SISKOWITT RIVER, 0.8 *m.* Here a bridge crosses the river, a little cascade runs (R), and the falls proper are hidden in a dense tangle of underbrush between two high bluffs a short distance downstream. The falls consist of a series of 15 rocky shelves down which the water breaks.

State 13 traverses a swampy region drained by the West Siskowitt River and Bark Creek, 48.9 *m.*, a small trickle down a wide flood plain originally cut by a mighty post-glacial river.

HERBSTER, 52.8 *m.*, is at the junction with a town road.

Right on this town road along the shore of the lake to the tip of BARK POINT, 5 *m.* The road, lashed periodically by waves and spray, is often littered with driftwood. A few cottages and taverns line the bleak roadside. Right is a high bluff that gradually slopes down to Bark Point; beyond it is the entrance to Bark Point Bay and (L) the vast expanse of Lake Superior.

PORT WING, 60.1 *m.* (250 pop.), is a declining little fishing village. Like Herbster and other lakeshore villages, Port Wing is a trade center for neighboring farmers, most of them of Finnish stock and still addicted to their traditional steam baths. Many farms in this region have square, air-tight, log bathhouses; occasionally a group of families erects a large bathhouse in common. Once or twice a week, summer and winter, entire families, scantily clad and carrying pails of water, troop out to the bathhouses. Benches and bunks line the walls of the bathhouses from floor to ceiling; water is poured on stones heated in a fireplace or open stove; soon the room is clouded with steam; stretched out on the benches, the bathers "cook" in the vapor.

The Finnish immigration into the Lake Superior region began about 1864 and increased greatly in 1878 and 1899. The Finns first settled as miners in the copper country of Michigan, near Hancock, then drifted slowly down to the Ironwood and Hurley region. In the early 1880's they began filtering into northern Wisconsin. Some found employment in the iron mines; others, like those at Port Wing, began to take up farms all along the route from Michigan to Minnesota. By 1900 they were permanently settled, forming the cooperatives for which they are famous (*see Cooperative Movement*).

West of Port Wing, State 13 crosses an area little changed since the first settlers arrived here in the 1850's. Crossing Iron River, 67.5 *m.*, the highway continues through other deep, narrow, wooded valleys that reveal glimpses of winding, spruce-dark lowland, crosses streams tinted red by the iron-bearing soil, passes shiny milk cans on crude platforms at the roadside, and traverses occasional strips of farmland. Beyond the Bois-Brule River, 77.4

m., which flows between wooded and almost perpendicular banks, the trees gradually thin out. Silos and wire fences are common now, farms are better kept. Big shedlike pea vineries stand at crossroads, each backed by a stack of stripped vines. At 95.2 *m.* is a large WINDMILL made of white cement, built in 1885 by Nicholas Davidson, one of the earliest of the Finnish settlers. Until 1918 flour and grist were ground here between stones that Davidson had cut by hand.

At 95.3 *m.* is the junction with County V.

Left on County V to JAMES BARDON PARK, 5 *m.* (*see Tour 14*).

At 99.7 *m.* is the junction with US 2 (*see Tour 14*) and US 53 (*see Tour 10*) ; between this junction and Superior, State 13, US 53, and US 2 are one route (*see Tour 10*).

SUPERIOR, 107.9 *m.* (629 alt., 36,113 pop.) (*see Superior*).

Superior is at the junction with US 53 (*see Tour 10*), State 35 (*see Tour 13*), and US 2 (*see Tour 14*).

Niedecker worked on this guide for the WPA.

[FOLLOWING: Niedecker's typed notes,
"Michigan State Guide 1941"]

State 35 -
    Old mining or lumber centers. Dense forests of cedar, birch
and poplar. Pines, beeches, blueberry plains.

Negaunee -   first discovery of iron ore in the Lake Superior region.
a 12 ft. pyramid of iron ore blocks erected in 1904 as monument to
discovery. which took place in 1844 by a group of explorers from
Jackson, coming here to mine copper, silver and gold.

Palmer - a charming little water fall

Escanaba River State Game Refuge - 2 miles or so from Palmer.
Princeton yielding heavy blueberry crops and The Princeton Mine.
Gwinn, a small town for mining employees on east branch of Escanaba
R.   Rock - The early settlers cut maple forests for the charcoal
kilns.

Gladstone - Industrial with deep water harbor on L. Michigan. Hard-
wood flooring, veneer and plywood

Escanaba (Ind. Land of the Red Buck) 14,000 pop in 1941, iron ore
shipping and paper and hardwood and commercial fishing. In 1936
Escanaba furnished 100,000 sq. ft. of bird's eye maple for the
Cunard lines S. S. Queen Mary. In April the annual Smelt Fishing
Jamboree. Smelt fishermen, clad in hip boots and carrying dipnets
march thru the streets in an opening torchlight parade. The river
banks during the dipping are lighted by torches and bonfires.

Ford River on Green Bay was an important lumber mfg. place. Now the
docks are rotting and the bay channels are filled with sand.

Fox now a resort.

Cedar River

Menominee   Last week in July sailboat races (Men. R.) Their smelt
celebration in April a huge thing. In 1934 2 fishermen lifted
(pullys etc.) 4.200 lbs of smelt in less than 5 hrs. At night during
these festivities fires are lit by auto tires gathered by the
theatres of the Twin Cities (Marinette is a twin) at 'Fire matinees
for children, the price of admission to the show is one old tire.
Marker at West End Park, 3 blocks w. of Interstate Bridge - War
between Menominee and Chippewa.

Manistique (Ind. vermilion) mfg. and resort - Manistique R. Started
with lumbering   car ferry between Green Bay and Manistique.

Thompson US 2 clear cold water - springs spouting way into the air.
In Big Spring no frogs or any animal life can live. Sand if brought
up to the air from the bottom, turns black.

Kipling and Rudyard   both named for Kipling by Gen'l Mgr. of Balti-
more and Ohio R. R. - railroads selling stock and securities to
 investors in British Isles.
    Rudyard - so many mosquitoes here in early days.
    Kipling - once a site of charcoal iron furnace and chemical plant.
Until timber was exhausted. The kilns, rounded beehives of stone,
and the idle docks the sign now of Kipling's old time prosperity.
    Kipling himself acknowledged the naming of the towns with a
photograph of himself and a poem on the back:

                'Wise is the child who knows his sire,'
                The ancient proverb ran,

over

But wiser far the man who knows
How, where and when his offspring grows,
For who the mischief would suppose
I've sons in Michigan?

Yet I am saved from midnight ills,
That warp the soul of man,
They do not make me walk the floor, -
Nor hammer at the doctor's door;
They deal in wheat and iron ore,
My sons in Michigan.

O, tourist in the Pullman car
(By Cook's or Raymond's plan),
Forgive a parent's partial view;
But maybe you have children too -
So let me introduce to you
My sons in Michigan.

003.19.056

On a Monument
to the Pigeon

ALDO LEOPOLD

We have erected a monument to commemorate the funeral of a species. It symbolizes our sorrow. We grieve because no living man will see again the onrushing phalanx of victorious birds, sweeping a path for spring across the March skies, chasing the defeated winter from all the woods and prairies of Wisconsin.

Men still live who, in their youth, remember pigeons. Trees still live who, in their youth, were shaken by a living wind. But a decade hence only the oldest oaks will remember, and at long last only the hills will know.

There will always be pigeons in books and in museums, but these are effigies and images, dead to all hardships and to all delights. Book-pigeons cannot dive out of a cloud to make the deer run for cover, or clap their wings in thunderous applause of mast-laden woods. Book-pigeons cannot breakfast on new-mown wheat in Minnesota, and dine on blueberries in Canada. They know no urge of seasons; they feel no kiss of sun, no lash of wind and weather. They live forever by not living at all.

Our grandfathers were less well-housed, well-fed, well-clothed than we are. The strivings by which they bettered their lot are also those which deprived us of pigeons. Perhaps we now grieve because we are not sure, in our hearts, that we have gained by the exchange. The gadgets of industry bring us more comforts than the pigeons did, but do they add as much to the glory of the spring?

It is a century now since Darwin gave us the first glimpse of the origin of species. We know now what was unknown to all the preceding caravan of generations: that men are only fellow-voyagers with other creatures in the odyssey of evolution. This new knowledge should have given us, by this time, a sense of kinship with fellow-creatures; a wish to live and let live; a sense of wonder over the magnitude and duration of the biotic enterprise.

Above all we should, in the century since Darwin, have come to know that man, while now captain of the adventuring ship, is hardly the sole object of its quest, and that his prior assumptions to this effect arose from the simple necessity of whistling in the dark.

These things, I say, should have come to us. I fear they have not come to many.

For one species to mourn the death of another is a new thing under the sun. The Cro-Magnon who slew the last mammoth thought only of steaks. The sportsman who shot the last pigeon thought only of his prowess. The sailor who clubbed the last auk thought of nothing at all. But we, who have lost our pigeons, mourn the loss. Had the funeral been ours, the pigeons would hardly have mourned us. In this fact, rather than in Mr. DuPont's nylons or Mr. Vannevar Bush's bombs, lies objective evidence of our superiority over the beasts.

This monument, perched like a duckhawk on this cliff, will scan this wide valley, watching through the days and years. For many a March it will watch the geese go by, telling the river about clearer, colder, lonelier waters on the tundra. For many an April it will see the redbuds come and go, and for many

71

a May the flush of oak-blooms on a thousand hills. Questing wood ducks will search these basswoods for hollow limbs; golden prothonotaries will shake golden pollen from the river willows, Egrets will pose on these sloughs in August; plovers will whistle from September skies. Hickory nuts will plop into October leaves, and hail will rattle in November woods. But no pigeons will pass, for there are no pigeons, save only this flightless one, graven in bronze on this rock. Tourists will read this inscription, but their thoughts will not take wing.

We are told by economic moralists that to mourn the pigeon is mere nostalgia; that if the pigeoners had not done away with him, the farmers would ultimately have been obliged, in self-defense, to do so.

This is one of those peculiar truths that are valid, but not for the reasons alleged.

The pigeon was a biological storm. He was the lightning that played between two opposing potentials of intolerable intensity: the fat of the land and the oxygen of the air. Yearly the feathered tempest roared up, down, and across the continent, sucking up the laden fruits of forest and prairie, burning them in a traveling blast of life. Like any other chain reaction, the pigeon could survive no diminution of his own furious intensity. When the pigeoners subtracted from his numbers, and the pioneers chopped gaps in the continuity of his fuel, his flame guttered out with hardly a sputter or even a wisp of smoke.

Today the oaks still flaunt their burden at the sky, but the feathered lightning is no more. Worm and weevil must now perform slowly and silently the biological task that once drew thunder from the firmament.

The wonder is not that the pigeon went out, but that he ever survived through all the millennia of pre-Babbittian time.

The pigeon loved his land: he lived by the intensity of his desire for clustered grape and bursting beechnut, and by his contempt of miles and seasons.

Whatever Wisconsin did not offer him gratis today, he sought and found to-morrow in Michigan, or Labrador, or Tennessee. His love was for present things, and these things were present somewhere; to find them required only the free sky, and the will to ply his wings.

To love what *was* is a new thing under the sun, unknown to most people and to all pigeons. To see America as history, to conceive of destiny as a becoming, to smell a hickory tree through the still lapse of ages—all these things are possible for us, and to achieve them takes only the free sky, and the will to ply our wings. In these things, and not in Mr. Bush's bombs and Mr. DuPont's nylons, lies objective evidence of our superiority over the beasts.

[FOLLOWING: From Niedecker's typed notes on
The Great Lakes Reader (1966, ed. Walter Havighurst)]

1846 - the lonely village of Sault Ste. Marie became a stirring place -
Discovery of the Cliff Copper Mine the year before brought a rush of
fortune seekers.

William Cullen Bryant visited here in 1846 - "The birch-bark canoe of the
savage seems to me one of the most beautiful and perfect things of the
kind constructed by human art." ".. when I looked at its delicate ribs,
mere shavings of white cedar, yet firm enough for the purpose - the thin
broad laths of the same wood with which these are enclosed, and the broad
sheets of birch-bark, impervious to water, which sheathed the outside,
all firmly XXXXXX sewed together by the tough slender roots of the fir-
tree, and when I considered its extreme lightness and the grace of its
form, I could not but wonder at the ingenuity of those who had invented
so beautiful a combination of ship-building and basket-work." 'It cost
me twenty dollars,' said the half-breed, 'and I would not take thirty
for it.'

Baleau and Mackinaw boat came between canoe and sailing ship. Bateau -
white man's adaptation of the bark canoe - of red cedar with a flat
bottom and pointed ends. Mackinaw - flat-bottomed with blunter ends
than bateau, constructed of red or white oak boards. Either could sail
60 miles a day with 20 persons and baggage and supplies.

At Quebec, 500 miles from Cape Gaspé, the river tastes of salt.

From the Writings of Pierre Esprit Radisson

1661

The month of August brings a company of the Sault, who were come by the river of the Three Rivers with incredible pains, as they said. It was a company of seven boats. We wrote the news of their arrivement to Quebec. They send us word that they will stay until the two Fathers be turned from [the] Saguenay [in order] that we should go with them: an answer without reason. Necessity obliged us to go. Those people [the Saulteurs] are not to be enticed, for as soon as they have done their affair they go. The governor of that place defends us to go. We told him that the offense was pardonable because it was [to] everyone's interest; nevertheless, we knowed what we were to do, and he should not be blamed for us. We made gifts to the wildmen that wished with all their hearts that we might go along with them. We told them that the governor minded to send servants with them and forbids us to go along with you. The wildmen would not accept their company, but told us that they would stay for us two days in the Lake of St. Peter, in the grass, some six leagues from Three Rivers.

But we did not let them stay so long, for that very night (my brother having the keys of the borough, being captain of the place) we embarked ourselves.

75

We [had] made ready in the morning, so that we went, three of us, about midnight. Being come opposite the fort, they ask who is there. My brother tells his name. Everyone knows what good services we had done to the country, and loved us, the inhabitants as well as the soldiers. The sentry answers him, "God give you a good voyage." We went on the rest of that night.

At six in the morning we are arrived to the appointed place, but found nobody. We were well armed and had a good boat. We resolved to go day and night to the River of the Meadows to overtake them.

Three leagues beyond the Fort of Richelieu, we saw them coming to us. We put ourselves upon our guards, thinking they were enemy, but [they] were friends and received us with joy and said that if we had not come in three days' time they would have sent their boats to know the reason of our delay. There we are in that river, waiting for the night. Being come to the River of the Meadows we did seperate ourselves, three into three boats. The man that we have taken with us was put into a boat of three men and a woman, but not of the same nation as the rest, but of one that we call Sorcerers. They were going down to see some friends that lived with the nation of the Fire, that now liveth with the Pouoestingonce or the Sault.

It is to be understood that this river is divided much into streams, very swift and small, before you go to the River of Canada. [Because] of the great game that therein is, the enemy is to be feared, which made us go through these torrents. This could make anyone afraid who is inexperted in such voyages. We suffered much for three days and three nights without rest.

As we went we heard the noise of guns, which daunted our hearts for fear, although we had eight boats in number; but [we] were a great distance one from another, as is said in my former voyage, before we could gain the height of the river.

The boat of the Sorcerers, where was one of us, albeit [had] made a voyage into the Hurons' country before with the Fathers.

The night following, [he] that was in the boat dreamed that the Iroquois had taken him with the rest. In his dream he cries out aloud. Those that were there at rest awakes of the noise. We are in alarm, and ready to be gone. Those that were with the man resolved to go back again, explicating that an evil presage. The wildmen counseled to send back the Frenchman, saying he should die before he could come to their country. It's usually spoken among the wildmen, when a man is sick or not able to do anything, to discourage him in such sayings.

Here I will give a relation of that Frenchman before I go further, and what a thing it is to have an intrigue. The next day they see a boat of their enemies, as we heard since. They presently landed; the wildmen runned away, the Frenchman also. As he went along the waterside for fear of losing himself, he finds there an arbor, very thick, lays himself down and falls asleep. The night being come, the wildmen being come to know whether the enemy had perceived them, but none pursued them, and found their boat in the same place and embarks themselves and come in good time to Montreal. They left the poor Frenchman there, thinking he had wit enough to come along the waterside, being not above ten leagues from thence. Those wildmen, after their arrivement, for fear spoke not one word of him, but went down to Three Rivers, where their habitation was. Fourteen days after, some boats ventured to go back for some oriniack, came to the same place, where they made cottages, and that within a quarter of mile where this wretch was. One of the French finds him on his back, and almost quite spent, his gun by him. He was very weak and desirous that he should be discovered by some or other. He [had] fed as long as he could on grapes and at last became so weak that he was not able [to go] any further until those French found him. After a while, being come to himself, he tends down [to] the Three Rivers. Where being arrived, the governor imprisons him. He stayed not there long. The inhabitants, seeing that the enemy, the hunger, and all other miseries tormented this poor man, and that it was by a divine providence he was alive, they would not have suffered such inhumanity, but got him out.

Three days after, we found the tracks of seven boats, and five yet burning. We found out by their characters they were no enemy's, but imagined that they were Ottawas that went up into their country, which made us make haste to overtake them. We took no rest till we overtook them. They came from Montreal and were gone by the great river, so that we are now fourteen boats together which were to go the same way to the height of the Upper Lake.

The day following we were set upon by a company of Iroquois that [had] fortified themselves in the passage where they waited [for the] Ottawas, for they knowed of their going down. Our wildmen, seeing that there was no way to avoid them, resolved to be together, being the best way for them to make a quick expedition, for the season of the year pressed us to make [an] expedition. We resolved to give a combat. We prepared ourselves with targets; now the business was to make a discovery. I doubt not but the enemy was much surprised to see us so in number. The council was held and resolution taken. I and a wildman were appointed to go and see their fort. I offered myself with a free will, to let them see how willing I was to defend them. That is the only way to gain the hearts of those wildmen. We saw that their fort was environed with great rocks, that there was no way to mine it. The mine was nothing else but to cut the nearest tree and so by his fall make a break and so go and give an assault. Their fort was nothing but trees one against another in a round, or square, without sides.

The enemy, seeing us come near, shot at us, but in vain, for we have forewarned ourselves before we came there. It was a pleasure to see our wildmen with their guns and arrows, which agreed not together. Nevertheless, we told them when they received a break their guns would be to no purpose; therefore to put them by and make use of their bows and arrows. The Iroquois saw themselves put to it, and the evident danger that they were in, but too late, except they would run away. Yet our wildmen were better footmen than they. There were Frenchmen that should give them good directions to overthrow them. [They] resolved to speak for peace, and throw necklaces of porcelain over the stakes of their fort. Our wildmen were dazzled at such gifts because the porcelain is very rare and costly in their country. Then seeing themselves flattered with fair words, to which they gave ear, we thrust them by force to put their first design in execution, but [they] feared [for] their lives and loved the porcelain, seeing they had it without danger of any life. They were persuaded to stay till the next day because now it was almost night. The Iroquois makes their escape. This occasion lost, our consolation was that we had that passage free, but [we were] vexed for having lost that opportunity and, contrariwise, were contented of our side, for doubtless some of us had been killed in the battle.

The day following we embarked ourselves quietly, being upon our guard for fear of any surprise, for that enemy's danger scarcely began, who with his furor made himself so redoubted, having been there up and down to make a new slaughter. This morning passes in assurance enough. In the afternoon two boats had orders to land some two hundred paces from the landing place. One took only a small bundle very light, tends to the other side of the carriage, imagining there to make the kettle boil, having killed two stags two hours ago, and was scarce halfway when he meets the Iroquois, without doubt for that same business. I think both were much surprised. The Iroquois had a bundle of castor that he left behind without much ado; our wildmen did the same. They both run away to their partners to give them notice. By chance my brother [Groseilliers] meets them in the way. The wildmen, seeing that they all were frightened and out of breath, they asked the matter and was told "Nadoue," and so soon said he lets fall his bundle that he had upon his back into a bush, and comes back [to] where he finds all the wildmen despaired. He desired me to encourage them, which I performed with all earnestness.

We runned to the height of the carriage. As we were agoing, they took their arms with all speed. In the way we found the bundle of castors that the

79

enemy had left. By this means we found out that they were in a fright as we and that they came from the wars of the upper country, which we told the wildmen, [and] so encouraged them to gain the waterside to discover their forces, where we no sooner came but two [Iroquois] boats were landed, and charged their guns either to defend themselves or to set upon us. We prevented this affair by our diligence and shot at them with our bows and arrows, as with our guns. They, finding such an assault, immediately forsook the place. They would have gone into their boats, but we gave them not so much time. They throwed themselves into the river to gain the other side. This river was very narrow, so that it was very violent. We had killed and taken them all if two boats of theirs had not come to their succor, which made us gave over to follow them, and look to ourselves, for we knowed not the number of their men. Three of their men nevertheless were killed. The rest is on the other side of the river, where there was a fort which was made long before. There they retired themselves with all speed.

We pass our boats to augment our victory. Seeing that they were many in number, they did what they could to hinder our passage, but all in vain, for we made use of the bundle of castors that they left, which were to us instead of gabions, for we put them at the heads of our boats and by that means got around in spite of their noses. They killed one of our men as we landed. Their number was not [enough] to resist ours. They retired themselves into the fort and brought [in] the rest of their [equipage] in hopes to save it. In this they were far mistaken, for we furiously gave an assault, not sparing time to make us bucklers, and made use of nothing else but of castors tied together. So without any more ado we gathered together. The Iroquois spared not their powder, but made more noise than hurt. The darkness covered the earth, which was somewhat favorable for us, but to overcome them the sooner we filled a barrel full of gunpowder and, having stopped the hole of it well, tied it to the end of a long pole, being at the foot of the fort. Here we lost three of our men. Our machine did play with executions. I may well say that the enemy never had seen the like. Moreover, I took three or four pounds of powder; this I put into a rind of a tree, then a fuse to have the time to throw the rind, warning the wildmen as soon as the rind made his execution that they should enter in and break the fort upside down, with the hatchet and the sword in their hands. In the meantime the Iroquois did sing, expecting death, or to their heels. At the noise of such a smoke and noise that our machines made with the slaughter of many of them, seeing themselves so betrayed, they let us go free into their fort that thereby they might save themselves. But having environed the fort, we are mingled pell-mell so that we could not know one another in that skirmish of blows. There was such an noise that should terrify the stoutest men.

Now there falls a shower of rain and a terrible storm that to my thinking there was something extraordinary: that the devil himself made that storm to give those men leave to escape from our hands to destroy another time more of these innocents. In that darkness everyone looked about for shelter, not thinking of those braves that laid down half dead to pursue them. It was a thing impossible; yet do believe that the enemy was not far. As the storm was over, we came together making a noise, and I am persuaded that many thought themselves prisoners that were at liberty. Some sang their fatal sang, albeit without any wounds, so we represent unto them, making them gather all the broken trees to make a kind of barricade, prohibiting them to cut trees, that thereby the enemy might not suspect our fear and our small number, which they had known by the stroke of their hatchets. Those wildmen, thinking to be lost, obeyed us in everything, telling us every foot, "Be cheerful, and dispose of us as you will, for we are men lost." We killed our four prisoners because they embarrassed us.

From the Writings of Henry Rowe Schoolcraft

1832

We resumed the ascent at five o'clock in the morning, (12th.) The course of this branch of the river, above the Kubbakunna Lake, resembles a thread wound across a savannah valley. A species of coarse marsh-land grass covers the valley. Clumps of willow fringe this stream. Rushes and Indian reed are gathered in spots most favorable to their growth. The eye searches in vain, for much novelty in the vegetation. Wherever the stream touches the solid land, grey pine, and tamarack are conspicuous, and clumps of alder here take the place of willow. Moss attaches itself to almost every thing. And there is a degree of dampness and obscurity in the forest, which is almost peculiar to the region. Water fowl seem alone to exult in their seclusion, and evince the infrequency of intrusion by flying a short distance, and frequently alighting within gun-shot.

After we had gone on a little more than an hour, the Indian in the bow of the forward canoe, fired at, and killed a deer. We all landed to look at the animal. Although fairly shot through the fore part of the body, it ran several hundred yards before it fell. The Indian traced it by its blood, and found it quite dead. He brought it to the banks of the river, before skinning it. We stood in astonishment at the dexterity with which this operation was performed. In a very few minutes it was disrobed of its skin, quartered and dissected. The owner presented me the quarters. He gave the *moze* to our guide. This term comprehends all parts of the carcass except the four quarters, head and entrails. Nothing was, however, thrown away; and we had occasion, at night to observe, that the aid of fire enables them, with very little of the culinary art, to despatch those parts of the animal, which, it might be inferred, were most in need of preparation. Signs of this animal were frequently seen, and had the objects of the journey permitted delay, it might have been often killed.

Our progress through the savannahs was rendered more unpleasant than it would otherwise have been, by frequent showers of rain, which gave, as is usual, a peculiar activity and virulence to the musquito. When the usual hour of landing for breakfast had arrived, the banks were too marshy to admit of it, and we went on until a quarter past twelve. We then again renewed a labor with little variety of incident.

At half past five we came to an elevated sand-hill on the right shore, covered with yellow pine, and presenting a naked face towards the river. As one of the canoes required mending, I directed the men to land at this spot, for that purpose. Oza Windib, who was a little in the rear, at the moment, said, on coming up, that we were within a few hundred yards of the junction of the Naiwa, the principal tributary of this fork; that a series of rapids commenced at that point, which would render it necessary to make a portage the whole extent of them, and that it was better to commence the portage at this place, as the river so ran, that we might go directly back through the forest, and strike its channel. He said that the Naiwa, which came in on the left, was a stream of considerable length, and originated in a lake [George] which was infested by copper-head snakes, to which its name has reference. I observed that the soil at this place was of a diluvian character, and embraced pebbles, and small boulders of syenite, trap rock, and quartz, and other debris of primitive and secondary rocks. One of the party picked up a well characterised piece of zoned agate.

While the mending of the canoes was in progress, the baggage was put in portable order, and as soon as all was ready, the men moved on with the canoes and effects, which were so arranged that all could be carried at one load, and it did not require them to go back. This was a point originally kept in view, in the curtailment of the baggage at the island, and it was an object of the highest importance to the speed and success of the trip. Each canoe and its apparatus, with some of the lighter pieces was carried by one man. The guide led off the men, with no slight burden on his own shoulders, first scrambling up the sandy acclivity, and then striking through a growth of scrub oak and pines. The showers of the morning had so thoroughly wet the grass and shrubbery, that a few moments walking through it, was sufficient completely to saturate both pantaloons and stockings. I walked out a few hundred yards from the trail, towards the left which brought me into the curve of the river, in view of the rapids. There appeared to be a series of small rapids, with intervening shallows. The noise of falling water and the white wreaths of foam, induced me to think there might be distinct falls, but I could discern nothing entitled to the name. The average descent of the river, at this series of rapids, appeared to be, however, considerable, and might perhaps be estimated at forty-eight feet. I rejoined the party at the spot they had selected for their first pause, somewhat to their relief, probably, as guns had been fired by them, under the belief of my having missed the way. We first came in sight of the river again, on the brow of an elevated sand-hill, precipitous towards the water. The guide halted to inquire whether it would not be preferable to encamp at this spot, as we should suffer less from insects than if we encamped in the valley of the river, at the termination of the portage. As the day light was not gone, and some distance still remained, I deemed it better to go on, that we might have nothing to do in the morning, but to put our canoes in the water. On reaching the bank of the stream, we found its current placid, and our guide informed us that we had now surmounted the last rapids.

A fog prevented our embarking until five o'clock in the morning, (13th) and it was then impossible to discern objects at a distance. We found the channel above the Naiwa, diminished to a clever brook, more decidedly marshy in the character of its shores, but not presenting in its plants or trees, any thing particularly to distinguish it from the contiguous lower parts of the stream. The water is still and pond-like. It presents some small areas of wild rice. It appears to be a favorite resort for the duck and teal, who frequently rose up before us, and were aroused again and again by our progress. An hour and a half diligently employed, brought us to the foot of Ossowa [As-sawa] Lake. We halted a moment to survey it. It exhibits a broad border of aquatic plants, with somewhat blackish waters. Perch abound in it. It is the recipient of two brooks, and may be regarded as the source of this fork of the Mississippi. We were precisely twenty minutes in passing through it. We entered one of the brooks, the most southerly in position. It possessed no current and was filled with broad leaved plants, and a kind of yellow pond-lily. We appeared to be involved in a morass, where it seemed equally impracticable to make the land, or proceed far by water. In this we were not mistaken; Oza Windib soon pushed his canoe into the weeds and exclaimed, *Oma, mikunna,* (here is the portage.) A man who is called on for the first time, to debark, in such a place, will look about him to discover some dry spot to put his feet upon. No such spot however existed here. We stepped into rather warm pond water, with a miry bottom. After wading a hundred yards, or more, the soil became firm, and we soon began to ascend a slight elevation, where the growth partakes more of the character of a forest. Traces of a path appeared here, and we suddenly entered an opening affording an eligible spot for landing. Here our baggage was prepared for the portage. The carbonaceous remains of former fires, the bones of birds, and scattered camp poles, proved it to be a spot which had previously been occupied by the Indians. The prevailing growth at this place is spruce, white cedar, tamarack and grey pine. We here breakfasted.

Having followed out this branch of the Mississippi to its source, it may be observed, that its existence, as a separate river, has hitherto been unknown in our geography. None of the maps indicate the ultimate separation of the Mississippi, above Cass Lake, into two forks. Little surprise should therefore be manifested that the latitude of the head of this stream, is found to be incorrect. It was not however to be expected that the inaccuracy should be so great as to place the actual source, an entire degree south of the supposed point. Such however is the conclusion established by present observations.

The portage from the east to the west branch of the river is estimated to be six miles. Beginning in a marsh, it soon rises into a little elevation of white cedar wood, then plunges into the intricacies of a swamp matted with fallen trees, obscured with moss. From this, the path emerges upon dry ground. It soon ascends an elevation of oceanic sand, having boulders, and bearing pines. There is then another descent, and another elevation. In short, the traveller now finds himself crossing a series of deluvial sand ridges, which form the height of land between the Mississippi Valley and Red River. This ridge is locally denominated Hauteur des Terres where it is crossed in passing from Lac Plaie to Ottertail Lake, from which point it proceeds northward, separating the tributaries of the River des Corbeau from those of Red River. It finally subtends both branches of the Mississippi, putting out a spur between the east and west fork, which intersects the portage, crosses the west or Itascan fork about the point of the Kakábikonce, or Little Rock Falls, and joining the main ridge, passes northeastwardly of Lac Travers and Turtle Lake, and is again encountered in the noted portage path from Turtle Lake to Red Lake. It is, in fine, the table land between the waters of Hudson's Bay and the Mexican Gulf. It also gives rise to the remotest tributaries of the river St. Louis, which, through Lake Superior and its connecting chain, may be considered as furnishing the head waters of the St. Lawrence. This table land, is probably, the highest in Northwestern America, in this longitude.

In crossing this highland, our Indian guide, Oza Windib, led the way, carrying one of the canoes, as his portion of the burden. The others followed, some bearing canoes, and others baggage. The whole party were arranged in Indian file, and marched rapidly a distance—then put down their burthens a few moments, and again pressed forward. Each of these stops is called a *posè* by the voyageurs, and is denominated Opugidjiwunon, or a place of putting down the burthen, by the Indians. Thirteen of these rests, are deemed the length of the portage. The path is rather blind, and requires the precision of an Indian eye to detect it. Even the guide was sometimes at a loss, and went forward to explore. We passed a small lake occupying a vale, about midway of the portage, in canoes. The route beyond it, was more obstructed with underbrush. To avoid this, we waded through the margins of a couple of ponds, near which we observed old camp poles, indicating former journies by the Indians.

The weather was warm and not favorable to much activity in bird or beast. We saw one or two species of the falco, and the common pigeon, which extends its migrations over the continent. Tracks of deer were numerous, but travelling without the precaution required in hunting, we had no opportunity of seeing this animal on the high grounds. It was observed in the valleys of the river, on both branches. Ripe strawberries were brought to me, by the men, at one of the resting places. I observed a very diminutive species of the raspberry, with fruit, on the moist grounds. Botanists would probably deem the plants few, and destitute of much interest. Parasitic moss is very common to the forest trees, and it communicates a peculiar aspect to the grey pine, which is the prevailing growth on all the elevations.

To the geologist, the scene is one of interest. The boulders of granite, and other primitive strata, occurring on the surface, remind him of the original position of these masses, in the system of nature and indicate revolutions affecting the earth's surface, which have widely changed both the position and form of these solid materials. When the soil itself is examined, it adds further evidences of such changes. We may refer its sand to consolidated strata of this mineral which have been broken down by oceanic action, and distributed in the remarkable ridges and elevations, which now characterise the face of the country. In whatever light the subject is viewed, it seems difficult to resist the conclusion, that water has been the cause, under providence, in effecting these changes, and that the highest grounds in this region, have been subjected to the peculiar influence which this element alone exerts in the work of attrition and deposition of strata, solid or diluvial. It might be interesting to inquire, in what manner this agent of change was withdrawn, and whether a current was created toward either of the cardinal points. It would aid this inquiry to observe, in which direction the debris and soils were deposited in the heaviest masses? How far granite boulders had been carried from their beds? And whether wood, bones, and other organic remains had been subjected to like removals? We think these accumulations are abundantly witnessed in casting the eye down the Mississippi valley, with a measured decrease in the size and weight of the pulverised masses, in proceeding from the head to the mouth of this river. It is thus evident, that the heaviest boulders are found on its upper branches, while they become rare in its central plains, and disappear altogether, long before its entrance into the deltas at its mouth. And this remark may be coupled with the accounts given by travellers of the bleak, and denuded, and sterile character of the northern rock formations.

But we have no leisure to devote to this investigation, and must proceed with the narrative that is before us. Every step we made in treading these sandy elevations, seemed to increase the ardor with which we were carried forward. The desire of reaching the actual source of a stream so celebrated as the Mississippi—a stream which La Salle had reached the mouth of, a century and a half (lacking a year) before, was perhaps predominant; and we followed our guide down the sides of the last elevation, with the expectation of momentarily reaching the goal of our journey. What had been long sought, at last appeared suddenly. On turning out of a thicket, into a small weedy opening, the cheering sight of a transparent body of water burst upon our view. It was Itasca Lake—the source of the Mississippi.

[FOLLOWING: Niedecker's handwritten
geology notes (pages 1 and 2 of 6)]

Azoic Time -
3000 - 5000 million yrs. ago - formation of earth

Pre-Cambrian Time - lasted 1000-1500 million yrs.

   Archeozoic era - much volcanic
   Proterozoic " - iron, copper - glacial
       periods at least twice
       simple marine life

Paleozoic Era - invertebrates and marine forms -
   lasted 300 million yr.

   Cambrian - began 505 million yrs. ago
     seas over most of world
     marine invertebrates — shells, calcareous
     marine algae. Some lichens.
   Ordovician - lasted 65 million yrs. - first
     primitive fish-like vertebrates
     deposition of marbles, limestones, slates
Silurian period → began 360 million yrs. ago
   lasted 35 million yrs.
   seas — great salt beds deposited
   great changes in US.
   Beginnings of land plants.
   Devonian period - began 325 million yrs. ago
   lasted 65 million yrs.
   Volcanic activity
   Age of fishes
   Wingless insects + spiders
   ferns, mosses, horsetails
   Tree fern forests + primitive evergreens
   Carboniferous — began 280 million yrs age. Lasted
   50 million yrs. Almost 80% of world's
   coal beds formed from marshy vegetation.
   Air warm + moist. Fish abundant.
   giant dragonflies.
   Permian — began 230 million yrs ago, lasted
   25 million yrs. Land rose. Widespread
   aridity — deserts formed. Reptiles + forked.
Mesozoic Era - Age of Reptiles — lasted 130 million yrs.
   dinosaurs, many bipedal. Vertebrate animals.
   Jurassic period — dinosaurs, reptiles
Cretaceous → chalk period coal + oil in
   western US. At close of this period

dinosaurs became extinct

<u>Cenozoic</u> Era – mammals & modern seed plants
15 million years, its length of period
Horse 1 ft. high
Paleocene + Eocene – modern birds. Seed-
bearing plants
Oligocene ⟶ mammals dominant. Cat &
dog families supreme. Primitive
anthropoid apes. Primates
walked erect
Miocene – volcanic activity – modern birds.
Great ape in Europe.
Pliocene – Land still rose. Horse evolved
almost to modern form. Manlike apes –
gibbon; gorilla. Beginning of Stone
Age ∴ earliest implements of
man, antedating any skeleton
of man himself thus far discovered.
Pleistocene – Glaciers – disappeared 2
N.Y. 38,000 yrs. ago & from Sweden
12000 yrs. ago. Great Lakes formed
when ice last disappeared. Four
species elephants in N.A. including
mastodon & mammoth, also camels,
sabretooth tiger. Camels & horse
survived glacial eras but died out
in U.S. before advent of man.
Beginning extinction of mammals
& rise of man. (Cro-magnon
man was known for cave paintings)
Recent – began 25,000 yrs. ago. Most
glaciers melted & lands became
warm, Deserts. Neolithic man
developed roughly 20,000 yrs. B.C.
Civ. begins – pottery, community life,
agriculture. Domestication of animals.
Copper & bronze age began 5000–2000
B.C. and Iron age 3000–800 B.C.

½ 003.19.274